HOPEFUL DESPAIR

to my beloved
family —
thank you.
for everything.

with love,
alyssa

HOPEFUL DESPAIR

UNEARTHING PURPOSE THROUGH SOCIAL IMPACT WORK

ALYSSA SKITES

NEW DEGREE PRESS

HOPEFUL DESPAIR

Unearthing Purpose Through Social Impact Work

ISBN

978-1-64137-435-4 *Paperback*

978-1-64137-436-1 *Kindle Ebook*

978-1-64137-437-8 *Digital Ebook*

CONTENTS

"One of the best things you can do for your own happiness is to think about something beyond yourself and see what you can do to create more joy in the world around you. The feeling of giving provides you with a reason for why you're going about your day and why you exist."

—CHRIS TEMPLE,
DIRECTOR AND COFOUNDER OF OPTIMIST

THE SOUL OF
THE FLOWER

———

The other day, I tried to write about a flower.

I sat down and attempted to describe in words how such a common feature of nature spoke to me. At the time, staring at it, I simply could not write. It wasn't until later, sitting at home in my bed, that I could.

When I had first seen this flower, I was perplexed, fixated on a thought so divergent from reality. This flower reminded me of myself. It was yellow, but not the bright yellow children use to color pictures of the sun—a color they use without yet understanding the verity of the world. This flower was not a vibrant yellow but rather a dirty shade of the color. While it may have once been the exact shade we often idolize sunflowers for, it had since been robbed of its brightness. It was clear that the flower had been stomped on, imprinted by the footsteps of many.

What fascinated me the most, however, was a speck on the left-hand side of one of the petals that looked as if it had broken through the musk, begging to tell me the story of how it used to shine. I left the flower feeling shadowed by an unexplainable curiosity. Was this little part of the flower shining through the last persisting fragment of what it used to resemble? Or was it the soul of the flower scratching its way out of the surrounding darkness?

The soul that is lit. The light that is spreading.

I used to live by the phrase "go out into the world and find yourself." However, the more I dip my toes into bodies of water that belong to worlds outside my own, the more I realize who I am is not something to be found.

I believe we are born as beings of the earth, engulfed in our innate authenticity. The older we become, the more we coat ourselves with doubt, anger, frustration, and sadness, all of which are products of the experiences we collect along the way. We do not need to live in the pursuit of finding out who we are because we are already ourselves: continuously imperfect and growing. I do believe, however, that change and the experiences it evokes are what allow us to become more aware of the elements of life that encourage us to shed off our self-imposed layers. By identifying these weights we carry for what they are, we can begin to rid ourselves of them and inch our way back to our truest selves.

I believe the same could be said about the birth of our purpose. Like my conviction of how to "find" myself, I used to think I needed to search in order to find my purpose. I looked for it everywhere except myself. I now surmise we are born with our sense of purpose because, when I presume I am doing something that could be defined as purposeful, I *feel* it within me. I feel a sense of ignition, like something inside me was just let loose and is now on a journey to an ecstatic state of liberation.

Even if this belief is not entirely true, because truth itself is relative, it is comforting to know, or at least trust, that everything you genuinely desire is already within you. Once you begin to dismiss others' perceptions of the meaning behind the yellow specks lathering your being, you'll be able to see them for what they truly are: bright lights that expose glimpses of the purpose within you. Lights that only shine when you believe they can.

HOW THIS BOOK CAN BENEFIT YOU

—

Find a story, any story, that connects to your soul. Not just the one that sends chills down your back, but the one that ignites something unexplainable within you. I want you to not solely read this book. Instead, I hope you find yourself in certain parts of it. Insert yourself in every situation and do not hold back for fear of being self-indulgent (It's okay. I'm giving you full permission . . . just do it!).

Put yourself into the chapters or scenarios that resonate with you. *Become* the social impact worker or the person being offered assistance and ask yourself how you would deal with that situation. Would you continue? Would you try harder? *Become* the individual and probe your own mind. How would you cope with that trauma or stress? Would you so fearlessly persevere?

Participate, learn, question . . . grow. That is all I ask. You have no right, however, to judge or discredit the very raw existence of any facets of this book you find yourself becoming. Instead, recognize the art of becoming without the act of replacement. You see, each individual in this book has a story, a dream, a life that must be respected.

Participate in this book by learning and questioning yourself. How do you fit into the works of the world? What is your innate purpose? How can you share your warmth with others? If you feel compelled to learn more about a certain organization described or feel the need to help them meet their goals, follow the citations within each story for more information.

You do not have to agree with everything in this book. Hell, you don't even have to agree with most of it. However, I beg you to allow your innermost self to reveal its cause . . . your cause. Believe in it, believe in yourself, and grow. Always be willing to grow.

THE WARMTH WITHIN

———

Blythe Hill was four years old the first time she was molested.

She confessed, "I have firsthand experience of carrying the shame, guilt, and questions about my own value. It took me years and years to truly unpack and heal from what had happened to me." Having gone through those horrors, she felt compelled to join the effort to stop others from enduring similar experiences. She just had to figure out how.

That was why, when Blythe first learned about the gravity and extent of human trafficking as an adult, she was hit so close to home. During college, she stumbled upon an article about sex trafficking in India and was horrified. How was slavery still occurring? From this repulsive thought, she felt a sense of urgency she had never experienced before. In a couple of years, she recognized the link between her passion and urgency for this issue and her own experience of sexual abuse.

In 2009, Blythe started a fun, personal challenge of wearing a dress every day during the month of December. She explained how she was in college and was feeling stifled by the academic routine and in need of a creative outlet. As someone who always got a kick out of puns, Blythe titled her little personal challenge Dressember, as a play on words based on the month in which it was initiated.[1]

The following year, to her surprise, some of her close friends informed her they would also like to participate in the style challenge. The year after that, in response to all of the pictures she and her friends had posted the previous December, many friends of her friends also wanted to join in.

In 2013, Blythe realized people were not simply humoring her. People actually liked participating in this challenge. The challenge had the potential to be more meaningful than a fun activity. Acting upon this realization, Blythe added an element of advocacy to Dressember, turning it into a fundraiser.

Using her disgust for the human trafficking crisis and her growing desire to be a force in changing it, Blythe reached out to the International Justice Mission (IJM), the largest anti-slavery organization in the world, to help her organize a fundraiser.[2] Blythe gathered everyone who had participated in the Dressember challenge the previous year and asked them if they would be willing to post pictures of their dresses every day to attract donations.

That first year, Blythe set the goal of raising $25,000—an objective she felt was extremely ambitious. She settled on using Instagram, her primary social media platform, in order to spread awareness and attract donations.

To her surprise, the financial goal was raised within the first *three* days of December. By the end of the month, the

---

1   "Dressember Foundation," accessed December 4, 2019, https://www.dressember.org.

2   IJM, accessed December 4, 2019, https://ijm.org.

campaign far surpassed anyone's initial expectations, raising a colossal $165,000. The following year, Dressember raised nearly triple that amount, totaling more than $462,000.

Seeing the tremendous promise of her campaign, Blythe decided to always prioritize transparency with Dressember's donors so she could be sure the money was going to the right place. A donation to Dressember always goes directly toward important grants to generate true change.[3]

Now years into the campaign, Dressember has reappropriated the dress "as a symbol of freedom and power; a flag for the inherent dignity of all people." Nevertheless, according to Blythe, the dress continues to mean different things to different people.

Today, Dressember continues to raise crucial funds for the IJM and other anti-trafficking organizations. As of March 2019, they have wrapped up their sixth campaign year and have raised roughly $7.5 million to date. Dressember also hosts a 5K race in dresses and ties in Los Angeles and other cities throughout the country that helps raise money and awareness for the cause.

In 2018, the 5K raised over $40,000. That money has gone toward a grant needed to fund the youth programs at the Coalition to Abolish Slavery and Trafficking (CAST), another partner organization focusing on effective survivor-centric approaches within the anti-trafficking movement. "These funds will go toward aiding young girls and women," Blythe explained, helping them "to restore their own sense of dignity." CAST's mission in using these funds is rooted in the deeply settled belief that every human being is inherently valuable.

---

3   "Donate." Dressember. Accessed January 11, 2020. https://www.
dressember.org/donate.

So many people who have been trafficked feel fragile and alone, unsure how to navigate a life of normalcy. Dressember and CAST aspire to create a healing space for individuals who have survived and to acknowledge the very act of surviving for what it is: a symbol of outstanding strength and resilience.

In another effort to expand the campaign, each fall, Dressember also launches a dress collection by partnering with Elegantees, a sewing center in Nepal.[4] The collection of dresses is ethically curated by Nepalese survivors of trafficking. Elegantees partners with an organization called KIN Nepal to connect with women who have been rescued or intercepted from human trafficking at the Indian border.[5] Once they receive care through KIN Nepal, they are empowered and equipped to learn a trade of their choice. The women who work at the sewing center in Nepal have all made the conscious decision to work there. These powerhouse women workers are paid a fair, living wage and are able to give back to a cause that personally affected them.

To Blythe, this part of the campaign is one of the most fun and beautiful elements of what they do, because it provides a way for survivors to make a living while practicing a form of resilience through advocacy. Blythe stated, "Currently, there are over five hundred women on the waiting list to work in our sewing center. We would love to be able to bring all of them off the waiting list and give them sustainable jobs." By stirring up more demand for these dresses, more jobs will become available for those on the waiting list.

---

4   "The Dressember Marketplace," accessed December 4, 2019, https://dressembershop.com.

5   "आफन्त नेपाल (KIN Nepal)," accessed December 4, 2019. http://www.kinepal.com/.

Looking at the larger picture, Dressember's initiative also educates donors on the overlap between passion and labor trafficking and the importance of ethical consumerism. To consider our own contribution to consumerism, we must all obtain certain knowledge about where our clothes come from and how they are made.

Blythe has embarked on several visits to field offices of partner organizations where she has seen the impact of their efforts firsthand. She identified the conversations she has had with various survivors as simply the "greatest privileges" of her life.

One of the many stories that continue to stick with Blythe to this day is that of a young girl from the Dominican Republic named Liana.

Liana was raised by her grandparents after her mother left when she was a baby and her father died when she was eight years old. After her father died, Liana's mother would visit her on occasion. Throughout the years, Liana's mother became an avid drinker and drug user, and her grandparents tried to prevent her mother from leaving and reentering her life as they saw how dangerous she was becoming.

When Liana was around fourteen years old, her mother returned to her life and told her she wanted to live with her again. She tried to convince her daughter she had bettered herself and was ready to assume the role of a mother. Liana was thrilled because she had always craved a relationship with her mother, so she agreed to move back in with her.

Within a few weeks of living together again, however, her mother and her stepfather enslaved her and, presumably for drug money, began selling her to men for sex.

Nearly every day thereafter, Liana was forced to have sex with older men at various discreet hotels in the area. During every assault, her mother stood watching, threatening to kill her if she did not follow through with the man's demands as he raped her.

One of Liana's most common abusers was her stepfather's boss. After one night with Liana, the boss took her home and declared that she would be his child bride.

This man's mother, upon meeting the quiet, scared-looking girl, questioned her and discovered the truth of what Liana had been through. Eventually, she helped Liana find her grandparents, who had been desperately looking for her the entire time she had been enslaved.

When Liana was returned to the loving arms of her grandparents, she told them everything. Her grandparents, furious and devastated, reported Liana's mother to the local police. Fortunately, the police found and arrested her. At this point, the government prosecutors brought the case to the attention of IJM. IJM worked diligently to find not just Liana's stepfather but most of the other men who had taken advantage of this small, innocent child.

Liana was treated by IJM's aftercare team, and they assisted her through trauma-focused therapy and provided tools that would help her to develop her full potential.

Liana now lives safely back with her grandparents and just recently finished seventh grade. She hopes to one day become a pediatrician and envisions her life full of opportunity instead of tragedy thanks to the help of IJM and the funds raised through Dressember that helped fund the resources necessary to her recovery.

When visiting a field office in the Dominican Republic, Blythe had the privilege of meeting Liana. Blythe describes her as a "sweet, quiet, joyful young woman. It was so difficult to reconcile that this was the same person who was attached to such a heavy and heart-wrenching story." Liana showed Blythe and the others at IJM and Dressember that true self-transformation is possible when a person is provided with the necessary space and resources for healing.

In the summer of 2018, Blythe traveled to India to visit some field offices. While in Mumbai, she and her team learned a lot about the issue of female infanticide. Female infanticide is the practice of killing or abandoning female infants between the ages of 0-1 in some nations because of their societally ill-preferred gender. According to the World Health Organization (WHO), in India, the average ratio of male to female birth is 1.05, meaning that 150 boys are born to every 100 girls.[6] The problem of female infanticide is huge in this country, primarily because girls are seen as an economic burden to some families. This huge issue leads to a shortage of young women in the country.

When young men approach marriageable age, this shortage of women prompts an unsolicited demand within the sex trafficking industry. Young girls are dragged into this industry, usually after being kidnapped or led to believe they have some viable job opportunity in a different area. Instead, these girls are often forced to marry an older man who entered the industry in search of a child bride.

Blythe met someone personally impacted by this industry when she was in Mumbai. This fourteen-year-old Indian girl and her mother had both been offered opportunities to work outside their hometown. At some point after the two moved, traffickers kidnapped the girl from her mother. They tried to

<hr />

6   Maria Thomas, "India's Preference for Boys Has Produced 21 Million 'Unwanted Girls,'" *Quartz India*, January 29, 2018, accessed December 4, 2019, https://qz.com/india/1191272/economic-survey-2018-indias-preference-for-boys-has-produced-21-million-unwanted-girls/.

force her to sign a marriage contract. The girl refused and, as a result, was detained for nearly six months. While she was detained, the little girl's parents contacted IJM. Together, they put pressure on the police to follow leads and take action to find her. Luckily, Blythe explained, "Due to her parents' active role as advocates, efforts were made that ultimately led to her timely rescue."

Although I was relieved to find out this little girl escaped her desperate situation, it made me think about all the less successful cases. Many families in India do not have the financial ability, political influence, or even the will to make such efforts. More pressure on local police forces is direly needed—not only to recognize human trafficking as a very real and urgent issue but to be proactive in diminishing its occurrence and truly enforcing consequences on those who participate in such industries.

Speaking with Blythe and hearing some of the stories of those impacted by the work that she, Dressember, and their partner organizations do, I felt two overwhelming emotions: despair and hope.

These two feelings, although clearly antithetical by nature, often arise as a pair. I felt a sense of despair when considering how serious and life-altering human trafficking can be and how hard it is to overcome. I felt overwhelming despair in hearing the numbers, the countless quantity of individuals who have been and are currently stuck in this evil cycle. This feeling is both normal and necessary in order to instill in us a right understanding of the extent and gravity of the situation.

Although the scale of the problem can easily overwhelm, I also was unable to ignore the sense of hope I felt after talking to Blythe. I felt hopeful because, although modern-day slavery is still widely practiced, I understood that much is being done to combat it. According to Blythe, "in the United States, it is slowly becoming a standard procedure to train law enforcement officials to adequately handle cases of human trafficking."

I felt hope in the fact that things *are* changing; movements are growing and are being recognized as momentous and effective. Traffickers are beginning to see repercussions they've never experienced before. Organizations like Dressember are spreading awareness of the issue and driving people to act upon their accumulating desire to be a part of the change that is brewing.

* * *

Have you ever felt it? The heavy blankets of despair, grief, or sadness woven by the hands of others? Have they ever covered you with them, trapping you inside a sphere of darkness? Has other people's pessimistic view of the world ever impaired your ability to rebirth your artless gratitude?

Through every stage of life, the world likes to show us previously hidden facets of itself. Places where we used to see a never-ending horizon are blocked by the choppy and arbitrary waves of fear, doubt, and hopelessness. The waves never seem to slow down . . . *life* never seems to slow down. We listen to society as it tries—and often succeeds—to convince us that the reality of the world is a dark and cold place.

Whenever this happens, whenever you start to feel and accept *this* feeling, realign your attention within you. You have a warmth inside you that will never *fully* die. Do not let the world try to take it from you, because it's yours, and it's unique. This same warmth produces the energy that settles the waves and clears your vision enough to discern the true depth of the sea—the sea that, as understood by the child, reaches far past the visible edge of the horizon.

Sometimes recognizing the humanitarian defeats all around the world can simply become too much to handle. All too often, the world can seem overshadowed by the negativity such suffering and hatred creates. It is easy to get lost in and discouraged by the tragedies happening every day around us. However, these emotions of despair cannot be discarded. Instead, we must allow ourselves to experience them in order to motivate our actions. Every once in a while, we need to be horrified by the world and the behavior of other human beings in order to inculcate a sense of human agency in ourselves. By focusing on the progress being made on such issues, you may begin to be liberated from the overwhelming despair of others' struggles.

The amazing people and their incredible work described throughout these pages can inspire you to find your own path of meaningful, purposeful, passionate work. Find ways to be inspired by people who are doing great work—not necessarily because you have something meaningful to contribute to their cause, but because it does something to help you understand yours. This process of fathoming the seriousness of the world can, in fact, change your outlook to a more optimistic one. Acting within your sphere of influence will improve your own mental health, relationships, and overall happiness as you grow and foster the inner strength that enables you to do your part in making the world a little bit brighter.

And when it all is too much, when the world shows you nothing but all that is ugly, hone in on the warmth within you. Allow it to radiate through you . . . let it *become* you.

Once you genuinely believe in the beauty of your own being, the world will strip down its walls and show you the beauty it, too, possesses. Then you will begin to understand; if you have this warmth inside you, so do others. It sounds so simple yet is so easy to forget in the times when despair finds its home within us. Once you transform your life's mission and seek to ignite others' flames so they can mirror your own, you will feel like the accomplished adult you always dreamed of becoming, but one who hosts the mind of a child . . . hopeful and free.

ILLEGAL LOVE

———

George Reginald Freeman was arrested for being gay when he was only twelve years old. His uncle, who was the first person he told, beat him up and called the police. Although only detained for three days, when released, George was shunned not only by the uncle who had turned him in but also by his own father.

Homosexuality is illegal in thirty-eight countries in Africa.[7] George was born in one of these countries: Sierra Leone. In 1808, Sierra Leone became a British colony.[8] In 1861, a law called Offences Against the Person Act was legislated.[9] This law is still intact today and criminalizes same-sex consensual relationships between two people, essentially deeming anal sex to be punishable by a minimum of ten years in prison.

---

7   Amnestyusa.org. [online] Available at: https://www.amnestyusa.org/files/making_love_a_crime_-_facts__figures.pdf [Accessed 4 Dec. 2019].

8   The Commonwealth. "Sierra Leone : History." [online] Thecommonwealth.org. Available at: https://thecommonwealth.org/our-member-countries/sierra-leone/history [Accessed 4 Dec. 2019].

9   Refworld.org. (2009). [online] Available at: https://www.refworld.org/pdfid/4a643e030.pdf [Accessed 4 Dec. 2019].

George commented on the reality of this law. "If you look at the legal interpretation of this law, it doesn't necessarily state the gender. However, for years now, people have used this law to criminalize gay people. This act is even older than the constitution [of Sierra Leone] because the constitution was not declared until 1991. Because of this, people tend to overlook the laws of protection stated in the constitution."

Sierra Leone does not have much of a divide between religion and state. In fact, according to George, once an individual is elected into a political office, they have to take an oath as either a Muslim or a Christian. As of 2019, seventy-eight percent of the country's population identified as Muslim and nearly twenty percent as Christians.

"So if you are Muslim, you have to lead the country according to what is said in the Qur'an. If you are Christian, you follow the Bible," George explained.

A judge, often affiliated with one of the dominating religious groups, is responsible for determining the detention sentences of those arrested for committing acts of homosexuality. The judge typically declares a sentence between ten years to life imprisonment.

However, not all cases of homosexual behavior are persecuted based on the Offences Against the Persons Act. The Christian church, in particular, uses other angles, such as labeling homosexual behavior as an indecent act against the order of nature, which is part of the Public Order Act.[10] George has researched and studied the way the government has twisted its laws to enforce illegitimate detainments. Through what he has seen and learned, George wholeheartedly

10   M, Meisenberg Simon. "Sierra Leone." *Max Planck Encyclopedia of Public International Law*, 2013. https://doi.org/10.1093/law:epil/9780199231690/e1351.

believes that separation between religion and state will allow the country to have "a conversation about implementing diversity and inclusion policies that is necessary in order to truly work toward having a just and cohesive society."

When an individual in Sierra Leone is known or suspected to be an LGBTQI (lesbian, gay, bisexual, transgender, queer, or intersex) person, the policemen almost immediately take sides, leading to a myriad of arbitrary arrests and detentions without proper investigation. In certain cases, this has even led to heterosexual detainments. "This most often occurs when a man is perceived as more feminine or when a woman is a little bit more masculine than most. If the police hear of someone who could even *potentially* be a homosexual, they use this to blackmail them," stated George.

In Sierra Leone's medical facilities, when an individual has a sexually transmitted infection, they are expected to bring their partner in so that both individuals can be treated accordingly. However, George explained that "the real reason why they do this is not with the intent to help but to actually catch whether the disease was spread during same-sex intercourse." If someone reports their disease to a medical doctor and it is discovered it was obtained through same-sex intercourse, then by law, the doctor has an obligation to turn them over to the police.

The more George began to learn about some of the injustices of his country's laws and regulations, the more he knew he needed to get involved. After he realized he was gay and would not be accepted by his family, he began to get involved with policy change and advocacy. While living in Sierra Leone at age fourteen, George worked with the International Educational Resource Network (iEARN).[11] The principal idea of the

---

11   iEARN Collaboration Centre. "iEARN Collaboration Centre." [online] Available at: https://iearn.org/ [Accessed 4 Dec. 2019].

organization's project at the time was to bring young people together to make a difference within their own community. George's specific role was to learn about activism and how to create a network of support.

After about two years, George realized that, although this organization and others like it were working on great projects, not many programs addressed issues around sexual orientation and gender identity. Once George realized this lack of focus on issues he was personally affected by, he tried to reason with the program coordinator and other people within the organization to create a program for the youth that would include LGBTQI people. "Unfortunately, they were all too focused on mainstream sexuality," said George, "which I think is not good, because it leaves so many individuals without knowledge of their kind of sexual health."

Eventually, the discrimination George felt and saw conducted toward those around him mounted to such a point that he realized he couldn't sit back and pretend everything was okay. He dreamed of starting an organization that used advocacy to push the government to understand the situations of the LGBTQI people in Sierra Leone. He held out hope that an organization like this would one day be able to get the police to act in a professional and humane manner.

In October 2007, George accomplished this goal by establishing an organization with a mission of fighting back against LGBTQI discrimination in the Mano River Union countries of Guinea, Liberia, and Sierra Leone as well as Africans living in Europe. The organization, assuming the name Pride Equality International (PEI), continues to stick to its mission today: "We are committed to creating a world that is free from discrimination and violence on the grounds of sexual orientation, gender identity, and expression."[12]

PEI's focus is divided into four principal categories: advocacy, asylum seeker and refugee assistance, research and documentation, and sexual health and rights. PEI advocates at both a policy level through engagement with government officials and a community level through education and awareness practices such as trainings, campaigns, debates, radio programs, seminars, and more. Advocacy is one of PEI's most pertinent focuses because George believes in the power of institutional change despite the difficulty in achieving it. As he puts it, "Advocacy is a really long-term project because it has to do with a change in mind-set, and people don't like to be told to change their mind."

With this reality in mind and to strengthen their advocacy efforts, PEI continuously documents and monitors violations of human rights against the African LGBTQI community, immigrants, asylum seekers, and refugees.

A refugee, as outlined in Article I of the UNHCR 1951 Refugee Convention, refers to someone who is currently outside their home country and has left it due to "fear of being persecuted for reasons of race, religion, nationality, membership of a particular social group or political opinion...[and] is unable or, owing to such fear, is unwilling to return to it."[13]

Members of PEI who specialize in research and documentation also record qualitative data by capturing stories

---

12   Pride Equality International. "Stop Discrimination, Embrace Diversity." [online] *Pride Equality*. Available at: http://prideequality. org/ [Accessed 4 Dec. 2019].

13   Refugees, U. (1951). *Convention and Protocol Relating to the Status of Refugees*. [online] UNHCR. Available at: https://www.unhcr. org/3b66c2aa10 [Accessed 5 Dec. 2019].

of those affected by homosexual discrimination in Spain, Belgium, and France: the countries in which PEI's European offices are located.

PEI assists African LGBTQI refugees and asylum seekers by providing emergency housing shelters. When individuals enter one of the European countries they work in, PEI presents them with the option of a two-bedroom apartment equipped with food for a temporary stay. Then PEI reaches out to their local African community to see if anyone can host the asylum seekers until the government or a different organization like the International Rescue Committee can assist them in finding a more permanent solution. PEI also provides welcoming programs that teach the LGBTQI asylum seekers about their responsibilities and rights with the institutions that provide them with relocation services. Additionally, PEI helps pay for the asylum seekers they work with to attend language classes. Classes like this are essential to bringing the newly arrived individuals closer to a level of language proficiency necessary, in many cases, to get a job.

Through legal assistance and guidance, PEI connects its clients to pro bono lawyers who can help them follow the UNHCR steps to gain legal refugee status. In certain cases, PEI also aids their clients with attestation, independent reports, and helps gather the required number of signatures occasionally requested to support their claims to refugee commissions and asylum courts.

Within PEI's programs in the Mano River Union countries, unlike the programs in their European locations, their work has to be incognito. "We have made some strides to make sure that LGBTQI people get access to HIV services, which include condoms, access to testing, and other things like that. But we are still facing huge challenges since the work we are doing is seen as illegal," highlighted George. For this reason, within Sierra Leone, Guinea, and Liberia, PEI does not have actual offices. In fact, George clarified, "We tend to do a security and risk mitigation plan to map out the potential risks before we actually implement any of our projects." Instead of offices, PEI rents temporary spaces in quiet, safe locations. At these offices, they do not post signs indicating what type of work they do, what population they work with, or the name of the organization itself. "We don't want to put ourselves or the people we help in any kind of danger," added George.

A couple of years after PEI was established, they received a grant award from MTV's Staying Alive Foundation. This organization supports PEI in spreading its teachings on sexual and reproductive health. The Staying Alive Foundation eventually asked to interview George. In the interview, they asked him about his life and the challenges he had to go through as a gay person in an essentially antigay country. This interview was presented in the Universal Periodic Review to shed light on the injustice in Sierra Leone.

The interview was later transcribed word-for-word and published in a local Sierra Leonean newspaper. After this story was released, George received very hostile, threatening messages from members of his community. Eventually, the local police caught wind of this story and arrested and detained him once again. When this happened, George's colleagues at PEI sent a statement about what had happened to him to all of the international media networks and organizations they were working with.

Soon after, someone from BBC International got ahold of George's statement and sent one of their correspondents to do an interview with him while he was in jail. When the Sierra

Leonean police force heard that the BBC was going to come and interview him, they immediately released him from detention. They knew that his story would go viral and cause a huge international backlash on the country.[14] "As soon as I was released," George said, "I told the BBC everything I knew because I needed to let them know about the severity of the situation."

Although he had been let go thanks to his international recognition, he did not feel safe or accepted in his own country. Before George had been arrested for the newspaper article, he had been involved in advocacy work in Spain as he frequently attended international conferences and worked on international cooperation projects with other organizations supporting LGBTQI communities. Due to his prior work in this European country, the Spanish government eventually heard of George's situation after BBC International released his story. In response, the Spanish government offered to grant him an emergency evacuation from Sierra Leone to Ghana. He went to Ghana for two months and two weeks to get a Spanish visa because Sierra Leone had no Spanish embassy of its own.

After receiving his Spanish visa in Ghana, George flew to Spain. "My case was different than most because I was very lucky. I had relations with Spain. If I didn't, I don't know if I would have ever gotten out of my country," he confessed. Within his first few months in Spain, George lived in a reception center for refugees in Madrid. From there, he was transferred to the Canary Islands. He stayed in Las Palmas for six months until he was kicked out of the reception center because it was only to be used temporarily. Upon this change, he decided to buy a one-way ticket to Barcelona.

---

14   BBC News. (2013). "'Homophobia' in Africa condemned." [online] Available at: https://www.bbc.com/news/world-africa-23033423 [Accessed 4 Dec. 2019].

When he first arrived in the Mediterranean city, he stayed with a family he knew for about two weeks. Afterward, he lived on the streets for a while until he got involved with volunteering with the Catalan committee of the UNHCR. "Thinking about it now, the UNHCR became my backbone. They put me back on my feet. They helped me put my CV together, got me to go to Spanish classes, and other things like that . . . this was truly a huge turning point in my life." The two people who gave him the most opportunities within the UNHCR to be part of their advocacy effort were the former director, Mr. Joan Reventós, and the fundraising and regional coordinator, Ms. Laura Esquivel Lallana.

George has lived in Barcelona ever since. He currently holds a variety of advocacy positions in his community such as coalition coordinator for the African asylum seekers and refugees network in Europe where he coordinates programs and activities for the coalition. In addition, George is a board member for Africa LGBT and an international human rights and justice grants advisor at The Pollination Project. Three hundred and sixty-five days a year, The Pollination Project "gives grants to change makers across the globe" with the goal of fostering "a more sustainable, just, peaceful, and compassionate world."[15]

Aside from all of those positions, George still manages to find the time and energy to lead and direct Pride Equality International. PEI is now a member of the European Asylum and Refugee Network and has been contributing to the European Asylum and Refugee Movement that started in 2019.[16]

---

15   Fraccari, M. (2019). "Micro Grants for Social Change | The Pollination Project." [online] *The Pollination Project.* Available at: https://thepollinationproject.org/ [Accessed 4 Dec. 2019].

16   Ecre.org. "European Council on Refugees and Exiles (ECRE) |." [online] Available at: https://www.ecre.org/ [Accessed 4 Dec. 2019].

As a member of this network, George and other advocates at PEI lobby with policymakers to establish more just laws for asylum seekers, immigrants, undocumented migrants, and refugees. George expressed his hope of one day having a completely unified system within the European Union. "We know this is not something to be done overnight, but we are optimistic about the future," he stated.

George firmly believes that he is doing the work he is meant to do. "I have suffered a lot. I have seen a lot of injustice throughout my entire life. Regardless, my philosophy of life is to do the right thing for the right reason for the benefit of all. One of the main things I want to do is speak out and be an authentic voice for the people. That is what makes me happy. And what makes me happy—you know, where I find joy—is when I actually help people get through a time of need."

George put his life in danger by speaking out and confessing that he was gay to a public audience. He could have hidden his truth to save himself, as many others around him did. But George knew that if he were to continue to shelter who he really was, he would never be genuinely happy. "As a gay person growing up," he expressed, "I felt that the society I was a part of excluded me in many ways. So I decided I wanted to be a voice for not only myself but the entire LGBTQI community."

George believes in the power of advocacy through personal stories of empowerment. He stated, "I don't like to be anonymous, because if people like me want our stories to be heard, we have to show ourselves to expose our suffering to humanity." When you hear a name or see the face of someone who has overcome something you are struggling with, you feel more connected to them. Even if you cannot necessarily relate to their difficulties, you may feel a deeper sense of sympathy in realizing we are all human and—in another life—what has happened to them could have happened to you.

George was so motivated by the anger within him that he catalyzed it into a source of power. "Through my experiences, through the series of rejections I have been through, all of the bullying and discrimination I have faced based on the color of my skin, my refugee status, or my sexuality, I have become angry. But advocacy has become my way of turning all of the anger I have within me into something positive," he stated thoughtfully.

George surprised me with his humility. His speech was full of sincere gratitude. He thanked me for spreading his words for more to hear, earnestly expressing how the retelling of one's story is, in fact, a form of advocacy in itself. After going back and forth a bit conveying our gratitude toward one another, I left the conversation renewed by his encouragement and infectious energy.

George truly understands the complexity and reach of advocacy. He has seen how speaking up about his past has opened up opportunities for him and for many others who have been shunned from the world simply because of who they were born to love.

George acknowledges, and showed me, that change has an often unpredictable and arbitrary ripple effect, spreading with every person who is touched by a story or statistic. When one person feels deeply for another human being, whether they know them personally or not, another drop in the pond is added, filtering into the hearts of nearly every individual this person chooses to tell. It can be slow at times, the way the ripples move, but this doesn't mean they aren't still advancing. Because they are, slowly but surely.

REVAMPING THE
CREATIVE MIND

——

For years, people always told Chris Temple that the most important thing in life was to follow his passion. To Chris, however, this was bad advice.

"Passion isn't something you are born with," he said. "It is developed over time and through experience."

Instead of using passion as his initial motivator to get involved with social impact work, Chris was fueled by a constant cycle of jarring facts followed by sobering realities. He began to live by a phrase coined by Dean James Ryan: "When you meet someone or something that makes you go, 'Wait, what? How is that still possible?'" you should act upon your curiosity to make a difference.

For Chris, this aha moment was hearing that 1.1 billion people around the world live in extreme poverty. At that point in his life, the feelings that overcame him when he heard this statistic were a combination of disbelief and curiosity. In other words, a "wait, what?" moment. It wasn't a passion quite yet. It wasn't until he began to act upon his desire to do his part in alleviating poverty that he began to develop a true passion for the work.

Chris believes there is rarely a single aspect of life motivating you day in and day out, but rather a flowing force that can be hard to pinpoint at times. In fact, in his opinion, the development of a passion is a cyclical process. "Begin with something that interests you," he suggested. "Explore it so much that it then develops into a path that motivates you. I think the cycle continues to repeat, fueling that sense of intrinsic motivation."

Chris began his career as a film director by accident. Acting upon an unexplainable curiosity provoked by his aha moment, Chris and his friend Zach Ingrasci traveled to Peña Blanca, Guatemala between their sophomore and junior years of undergraduate college. For about two-and-a-half months that summer, they lived in a small hut and worked as radish farmers. They tried to live within this community on one dollar a day. Chris did this not necessarily with the intention of helping but rather to put himself in a position to learn.

Chris and Zach solely experienced a glimpse into what life was like every day for an average Guatemalan. As of 2017, over half the population lives under two dollars a day. However, in Peña Blanca specifically, the majority of the population is living under a minuscule one dollar a day. As a predominantly poor country, many Guatemalans face barriers that inhibit their access to adequate education, health care options, and more. In fact, school life expectancy is eleven years, as university is not always an option or even a thought. The contraceptive prevalence rate is only 60.6 percent due to a lack of contraceptive methods made available to the general public and the general absence of awareness. The low contraceptive prevalence rate partially contributes to the country's high birth rates and their status as the most populous nation in Central America. In addition, as Chris soon discovered the hard way, the risk of major infectious diseases is exceedingly high. The most common diseases include bacterial diarrhea, hepatitis A, and typhoid fever.[17]

After an extremely eye-opening summer, Chris described the day they left Peña Blanca as the most difficult part of the entire experience.

"I had lost about twenty-two pounds, had stomach parasites from the lack of clean water, was covered in flea bites . . . and then I got to go home. I remember walking into a grocery for the first time and feeling guilty at the excess and the lack of consciousness around separating our needs from our wants." Chris felt overwhelmed by how fortunate he was compared to those he'd spent an entire summer befriending in the impoverished community. He had to take a step back and reflect on his experience by asking himself, *What can I do with what I have and where I am?*

Throughout their summer in Guatemala, Chris and Zach filmed short video blogs so that their friends and family could follow along with their journey through Facebook and YouTube. Upon returning home, they realized they could actually do something incredible with all of these amazing videos that captured a glimpse of life in Peña Blanca. It dawned on them that they could give back to the community that had taught them so much by making a documentary film to inform the general public about how people lived in this community, which Chris knew was "an unimaginable reality for so many."

---

17   Cia.gov. "Central America: Guatemala." *The World Factbook - Central Intelligence Agency.* [online] Available at: https://www.cia.gov/library/publications/the-world-factbook/geos/gt.html [Accessed 4 Dec. 2019].

The actual creation of the documentary took them two years and sixty-five different versions. The final cut of the film was titled *Living on One Dollar*.[18] This documentary, which eventually reached a large audience after it was picked up by Netflix, has now gone on to impact countless people. The team that contributed to the creation of this film eventually realized the potential the documentary opened up and decided to establish a nonprofit organization called Living on One.

Living on One's mission was to focus on the use of film to advocate and raise money for issues of significance. Now, after seven years, Chris and Zach have decided to change the name of their nonprofit to Optimist. Chris explained this change in name. "Through our films, we are constantly meeting people who are fighting for something better. They have shown us that it is not naive to believe progress is possible."[19]

Optimist seeks to explore complex issues through the filming of intimate human stories. As of November 2019, Optimist has created six short films, one virtual reality experience, and two full documentaries: *Living on One Dollar* and *Salam Neighbor*.[20] For each film they create, the organization partners with a local nonprofit that serves and directly supports the communities featured in their films.

Through the generosity of donors all across the country who were touched by *Living on One Dollar*, Optimist has been able to raise over $1.5 million to support the community of Peña Blanca. Any profits from the film go straight to supporting these campaigns and events and has amplified

---

18 *Living on One Dollar*. (2012). [Film] Directed by C. Temple, Z. Ingrasci, and S. Leonard.

19 Optimist. Optimist. [online] Available at: https://optimist.co/ [Accessed 4 Dec. 2019].

20 *Salam Neighbor*. (2015). [film] Directed by C. Temple and Z. Ingrasci.

the process of retelling the individual stories. As of October 2019 in Guatemala specifically, Optimist's awareness and funds have provided 6,242 women with business loans (most from Peña Blanca), 500 homes with clean drinking water, 110 students with scholarships, and one new preschool and nutrition center.[21]

The sense of guilt Chris felt was alleviated slightly by creating this educational documentary and providing tangible help to the people in Peña Blanca. However, he still felt a bit at odds with the consumerism confronting him on a daily basis at home. He delineated, "For me, the best way to deal with the guilt I felt when I went back home was to stay connected to the stories of the people we met there. Yes, it was a two-and-a-half-month experience, but the relationships lasted so much longer than that." Chris still keeps in touch with many of the people portrayed in the film through Facebook.

In addition, Chris goes back down to Guatemala at least once or twice a year to strengthen the relationships he built there. "It has been one of the most rewarding parts of my job: to be able to develop these deep friendships over a very long time with people living [on one dollar a day]," he confessed. The authenticity of the relationships both Chris and Zach have with their friends in Peña Blanca is very evident even in the film. These relationships truly transformed the quality of the documentary. The more they were able to get to know the individuals, the deeper their understanding of poverty became. They realized, and portrayed in the documentary, that poverty is much more than a number or the surface-level academic definition people hear in the media or at school.

21   Optimist. Optimist. [online] Available at: https://optimist.co/ [Accessed 4 Dec. 2019].

Poverty is really about the individual people and what is holding them back from achieving their hopes and dreams.

One of the individuals Chris and Zach got to know very well is a lady named Rosa.[22] Rosa suffered from the effects of a very narrow perception of gender. By the age of seventeen in Guatemala, 75 percent of girls drop out of school, and Rosa was no exception. In fact, when she was only fourteen years old, she left school and experienced a very traumatic event. She was raped by a man she thought was her friend. He disappeared, leaving her to confront her conservative parents about her subsequent pregnancy. When she told her parents, they kicked her out of the house, leaving her without a chance to go back to school. To add to the pain, her parents informed her they thought her brothers were a better investment than she was.

Despite the lack of parental support, Rosa decided to keep her baby. When she gave birth, her daughter had hydrocephalus, which is a condition of increased pressure within the brain due to a buildup of cerebrospinal fluid. Rosa's daughter died after two years and nine months due to complications that arose from her condition.

In the face of everything Rosa went through, she still had a burning desire to one day become a nurse and give back to her community through medical support. At age twenty-seven, she was offered a microfinance loan of about $200 from a partner nonprofit organization of Optimist called Whole Planet Foundation. Whole Planet Foundation works to empower some of the poorest people in the world through microfinancing.[23]

---

22 Optimist. *Rosa - These Storms - Optimist*. [online] Available at: https://optimist.co/films/rosa-these-storms-documentary/ [Accessed 4 Dec. 2019].

23 Whole Planet Foundation. "Home." Whole Planet Foundation. [online] Available at: https://www.wholeplanetfoundation.org/

Rosa used the loan to start her own business selling hand-crafted woven fabrics. It was with this loan and the profits she made through her business that she was able to put herself back in school. At age twenty-seven, Rosa completed the years of high school she missed and eventually went on to attend nursing school.

In spring 2019, Rosa was one semester away from graduating. Her educational success can be attributed to the very small loan that led to a plethora of opportunities. In many ways, this is just one example that proves how poverty is defined by a lack of opportunity, not just a lack of money.

Chris remembers asking Rosa one day how he could "help her help herself." He is a firm believer that everyone has the strength within themselves to generate their own life-altering change. After all, as Chris puts it, "People are the only experts in their own lives."

When he asked Rosa this question, she said she didn't just want money, she wanted a market in which she could sell her fabrics. In response to her request, Chris and Zach started making T-shirts that incorporated her fabric into the pockets and began selling them on their web page. After *Living on One Dollar* hit Netflix, thousands of people began buying the T-shirts featuring her woven pockets. The demand for her shirts rose so dramatically that she ended up hiring twenty-one people in her home community to join her business.

Chris is so proud of the progress Rosa has made. "It's been a real pleasure to watch her take control of her life and build a better future for herself. And through that, her community is benefiting as well," he remarked. Rosa now facilitates trainings all over the community and gives talks to women about cervical cancer, maternal issues, and how to take better control of their health. She is able to offer insights that will change the lives of other individuals through her own experience of suffering and resilience.

Chris expressed how he has learned so much from people like Rosa who have lived completely different realities from his own. "I often say that people fear what they don't know, and that is why I think it is so important to hear from and forge friendships with people who are from different backgrounds, religions, sexualities, whatever it may be, to understand why other people live life the way they do."

Optimist has a new feature documentary coming out in 2020. After a decade of friendship and filming with the community of Peña Blanca, Chris hopes this new film will provide the kind of nuance and intimacy that makes a documentary truly memorable.

* * *

Chris separates his sources of inspiration for Optimist into two big driving forces: impacting the lives of the people around him and finding creative spaces to make art. He added, "My life has become this blend of these two things, creating documentaries into these pieces of art that can create an impact." Chris has looked for inspiration in both of these avenues to recognize his own sense of purpose.

However, some days it is hard to find motivation—days where you feel burned out from hearing story after story of the hardships endured by those experiencing abject poverty. The way Chris has dealt with this in the past is to focus on the individuals whose lives have been transformed as a result of his efforts. More specifically, the efforts of Optimist.

A filmmaker like Chris receives a lot of pressure to only look for inspiration from watching other documentaries.

However, he often finds that by exploring other creative fields with less pressure for comparison, it can be easier to discover his inner inventiveness again. He looks beyond his own areas of expertise to other products of creativity such as books, music, and visual arts. He sees how other artists portray their work and uses it as motivation to re-encounter his creative vision. He reflected, "Sometimes, you pour your whole heart and soul into your artwork, and afterward, you might feel a little empty and left with the question of what to give or create next. It takes a moment to recharge those batteries and find a new creative vision for yourself. And everyone's way of doing that is going to be different."

Most people can relate to what Chris has experienced, needing to look for inspiration to reignite their creativity. In those moments—through the pauses in the creativity that so organically flows through your veins—you must actively search for stimulation in everything and everyone you encounter.

The other day, I was struggling to find inspiration for this very book—a book that I consider a vessel for advocacy and awareness like Chris's films. While writing, I had evidently piled too much on my plate. I was working five days as a barista at a restaurant and interning the remaining two days of the week at a local refugee resettlement agency. Although I enjoyed both positions, I scarcely had a day off to fully rejuvenate physically or emotionally. This was happening during the time I was supposed to be finishing my manuscript's first draft. I tried and tried to write, but the thing is, you cannot force creativity.

Creativity and inspiration are floating and often fleeting sources of energy. Sometimes, the harder you force them to come to you, the further away they will float. They are electric, these energies, but you see, they must find a stable home to energize them in order to function.

That is why you, the person attempting to create or to be inspired, must make room for such energies. The more you free yourself from the barriers (negative mind-sets, sleep deprivation, or other detrimental practices), the more space you will have for creativity and inspiration to enter your being. It comes and it goes, but being inspired by your own life is how you will find yourself the freest to accept what ignites your inner expressiveness.

Recognizing the barriers I had created, I knew I had to rid myself of them if I was ever going to write this book. In other words, I knew I needed to lift myself from the stagnant state I had been swimming in for far too long. Whenever I get into states like this, when life seems too monotonous and uninspired, I always try to think back to the times I have felt freer . . . weightless, perhaps. For a long time, traveling has been that for me—exploring in a fashion that not only presents opportunities to experience newness in both people and places, but begs for it.

In response to all this chaos and knowing in my head, I decided to book a ticket to Portland to embark on my first-ever solo trip. I went on this trip with three simple goals in mind: to attempt to cure my own self-inflicted lassitude, to be curious in every moment, and to remind myself of the beauty that can be found in solitude.

I stayed at a little hostel called the Travelers' House. It was very homey and welcoming: the perfect place to first rest, then revamp my creative mind. Being alone allowed me to get out of my comfort zone and have conversations with other travelers that lit the same spark of curiosity and wonder I had been longing for. It was interesting, I noticed, how the conversations one has with other travelers seem to be fuller. For they are often stacked to the brim with animated storytelling—no restraints in talking about past travel experiences and, perhaps the most wonderful of all, the pure mutual eagerness to learn and to be amazed.

On the first day I arrived in Portland, I sat in Pioneer Courthouse Square waiting for the next bus to arrive. As I waited with my luggage sitting promptly beside me, I wrote my first journal entry of the trip.

I already feel it: the excitement of entering a new city and the uncertainty of traveling alone. I don't know what is to come this week, but something within me tells me it will be simple but meaningful.

Although not every moment of this mini trip was perfect, it was exactly what I had hoped for: simple yet meaningful. It was meaningful because it brought me back to *the* feeling that sheds light on the beauty that can be found within this existence when your mind and soul are set free. This feeling was similar to the one I got as I carelessly rode camels in the Sahara Desert to the place I would camp under moonlit stars. The same feeling I got rushing through the trees on a zip line in Croatia as my long hair floated swiftly behind me. The feeling I got as I hiked part of the Camino de Santiago with bubbling anticipation for what the next town would have in store.

This feeling makes me feel alive and inspired by what I am doing in the current moment. It takes me away from all that is dark and hopeless and brings me, if only for a moment, into a world that hosts nothing but light.

For me, this feeling clears space in my mind and heart for flows of creativity and inspiration to come flooding in. This feeling may be provoked differently for every person. Maybe it's jamming in your garage with your closest friends that does it for you. Or losing all sense of time and reality as you indulge in your next sci-fi fantasy novel. Or, maybe, you find it as Chris does through interactions with other individuals or from enjoying the products of various art forms.

And if right now, reflecting on your own interests and passions, you are struggling to find what your personal antidote for stagnation may be, consider what truly makes your heart ache with joy and your eyes light up with life. Once you recognize the very thing that sends waves of electricity through your veins, chase after it with everything you have.

But how does any of this relate to social impact work or the ability to avoid emotional burnout? If you leave no room for the electric charges of creativity and inspiration to radiate through your being (in other words, if you do not make a home within yourself), how could you ever wholeheartedly help others reach their personal state of desired bliss? If you, the alleged "social impact worker," the person volunteering, or whatever it may be, are not inspired by the work you are doing and the life you are living, you will not be able to benefit others in the way a brighter version of yourself could.

When you pass off this inspiration and love of life to those you aim to help, you are partaking in one of the most radical forms of empowerment. The relationship between Chris and Rosa is evidence enough. You are capable of so much more than merely "helping others." You have the power within you to be a living, breathing example of what it means to be a human who struggles but nevertheless persists with a positive and trusting sense of being. You have the potential, if you aren't already, to be a result of what is created when you breathe life into an otherwise soulless existence.

Therefore, the most practical and painless way to avoid emotional distress when helping others is to love your own life's cause so very deeply. It can be as (seemingly) simple as that. With the love you have for what you do, you can spread that in every interaction, every donation given, every meal delivered . . . every film made. And believe me, they will feel it. And maybe, just maybe, they will reflect some of the same love and kindness back to you.

FLOWERS AS A VESSEL FOR KINDNESS

———

In July 2007, Larsen Jay fell nearly two stories from a ladder he was using to do work on his roof. He fell flat on his face, leading him to spend several months in the UT Medical Center. He had a long list of injuries from this accident, including a broken left arm, left wrist, right wrist, right elbow, right femur, nose, and ten skull fractures. Although his days in the hospital were long and mundane, Larsen received an immense amount of love and support from his friends, family, and coworkers in the form of regular visits and gifts of flowers.

Larsen explained the transformative power of these floral gifts. "Within days of being in the hospital, my entire room transformed into a jungle of flowers. This jungle not only lifted my spirits but also served as a source of motivation to push through the series of surgeries and long hospital days I had to endure during my recovery."

One day in the hospital, Larsen asked his family and one of his nurses if they could help him get into his wheelchair so he could go outside to get some fresh air. As he was wheeled down his hall, he examined each room he passed. The principal difference between his room and the rooms of his hall mates was evident right away: his was painted with flowers and visitors while theirs were not. Without hesitation, he decided to distribute the flowers that were gifted to him to those in his hall. "Each patient lit up with the acknowledgment they received from me and the joy the flowers brought to their otherwise dark and dreary rooms," remembered Larsen.

Around six months after Larsen was released from the hospital, he, his wife, and some of their friends decided to replicate this act of giving flowers to patients in their local hospital. The pure joy scattered across each pair of eyes as they handed patients flowers gave them the assurance of the value of their work. They realized that this was something they needed to continue to do.

At the time, Larsen had a busy career as a film and television producer but decided that he wanted to create an organization that facilitated interactions with patients in need of a boost. From this idea bloomed the organization that is still growing today, Random Acts of Flowers. As the organization grew, they started an initiative to recycle and reuse old vases to prevent them from entering landfills where they would sit useless. The flowers they distribute have all been donated from weddings, special events, funerals, grocery stores, and florists.[24]

Larsen was full of stories from the times he'd delivered a vase of flowers, and it gave him joy to see patients' will to keep fighting. One of the stories that stood out to him in particular occurred in July 2011, about three years into the program.

---

24 Random Acts of Flowers. "Random Acts of Flowers." [online]
Available at: https://randomactsofflowers.org/ [Accessed 4 Dec. 2019].

A nurse at a hospital they partnered with called Larsen. She informed him that a lady she took care of was in desperate need of some kindness and interaction with another human being. When Larsen arrived at the hospital, he was told that the woman was ninety-four years old and had less than one week left to live. The nurse told him that the lady hadn't received any visitors in a long time, and it didn't seem as if anyone was coming anytime soon.

When Larsen entered the old woman's room, he approached her with the flowers, saying that he brought them for her. She tried to shoo him away, insisting that he must have made a mistake, that the flowers were surely not for her. As he tried to assure her that, no, he'd made no mistake, she denied him for a second time, telling him he must have gotten the wrong room. At a third attempt, Larsen simply handed the lady the flowers and explained who he was and why he was delivering flowers. The woman cried as it dawned on her that someone had taken time out of their day to hand-deliver her flowers and engage in an actual conversation with her about something other than her deteriorating health.

Her next words assembled the last push that caused Larsen to realize he wanted to do this full time. The dying lady looked at him and said, "You don't understand how much this means to me . . . no man in my entire life has ever given me roses before." And just like that, Larsen made a larger impact on this lady's life than he could have ever anticipated. He gave her a memory of love and kindness to hold on to while she lived out her last few days on earth. He left her feeling noticed and cared for when no one else had.

Shortly after this eye-opening encounter with the ninety-four-year-old woman, Larsen decided to quit his job in the entertainment industry and dedicate all of his time and effort to Random Acts of Flowers. Through this life-altering step, he was able to help lead the expansion of the organization. Currently, their home office is in Knoxville, Tennessee, and they have branches in Chicago, Illinois; Indianapolis, Indiana; and Tampa Bay, Florida. The entire staff of Random Acts of Flowers hopes to continue to bring their work to other cities and towns across the nation while maintaining the heart of the operation. To do this, Larsen hopes to instill in each location and volunteer staff member the purpose of what they do: the simple and meaningful human exchange of kindness and support.

As of 2019, Random Acts of Flowers has distributed close to five hundred thousand flowers to hospital patients. "We use flowers as a vessel of kindness that allows us to affect people from all sorts of backgrounds, ethnicities, and social standings," stated Larsen. He remembers giving flowers to another patient who hadn't received any visitors since the day he arrived. This man appeared to be very poor and, as observed by the nurses, perhaps had been living on the streets.

This man had been at the hospital for quite some time, spending day after day all alone. After receiving the flowers, he looked up at Larsen and simply but memorably remarked, "Thank you for remembering me." Through Random Acts of Flowers, this man felt recognized, perhaps for the first time during his hospital stay and potentially even long before that.

Larsen realized that flowers can cut through all types of barriers, even disabilities. One day, a nurse recommended that Larsen deliver flowers to a blind woman who had been situated at the hospital for quite some time. As Larsen entered the room, a bit nervous and unsure, as he had never delivered to a person who could not see before, the woman stopped him in his tracks. She smelled the flowers and immediately smiled. "Those are stargazer lilies!" she exclaimed.

After speaking with the grateful lady, Larsen discovered that she used to be a gardener. As he left her room, she thanked him for giving her a piece of her garden back. Larsen left feeling full and amazed. "It was astonishing to see firsthand how a little act of kindness can not only lift someone's spirits but also has the ability to bring back a memory, or a feeling, that had been long forgotten," reflected Larsen.

Larsen made a statement that remains the essence of Random Acts of Flowers' mission: "I changed my focus from success to significance." So many of us think of our futures and often equate our future success to the money we will make, the car we will drive, or the fame we will achieve. We dream high and hard with the hope of one day "making it." From hearing stories like Larsen's, I can't help but question what "making it" even means. When are we successful enough, and who determines that? We may get stuck in a cycle of disappointment when all we do is live our lives trying to become someone else.

By changing our focus from success to significance, the value of our existence will no longer be lost after we are gone. For the positive impact we've made on the lives we've encountered will live on far beyond us. The value of our lives will be shown through the footsteps we leave, the impact we make on the world around us, and the people that call it home.

REIGNITED

———

Michael Miner found time for fulfilling, voluntary work alongside a booming career as a screenwriter and large-format landscape photographer. Michael went to UCLA for a Bachelor of Arts degree in English literature and theater and a master's degree in fine arts. Throughout his nearly thirty-year career in screenwriting, Michael is probably best known for his movies *RoboCop* and *Deadly Weapon*.

Michael had a busy career, so I was surprised to hear about something he did for nearly eight and a half years of his life. Besides teaching screenwriting at a variety of institutions, including the Southeastern Media Institute and the University of California at Santa Barbara, Michael felt called to join InsideOUT Writers in Los Angeles.

InsideOUT Writers teaches creative writing skills in juvenile detention centers to inspire personal growth and empowerment, aiming to reduce the overall juvenile recidivism rate. The idea is to have professional writers go into these centers and teach the incarcerated youth crucial skills to help them reintegrate into communities after their release. The ultimate hope is to encourage the individuals to truly *want* to change the trajectory of their lives.

InsideOUT was founded back in the early nineties by a Catholic nun who recognized the problems of the nation's incarceration system.[25] Annually, the US government spends around $182 billion per year on mass incarceration.[26] Ryan Lo, a man who lived over twenty-three years in the California department of corrections, says that in the US, "Mass incarceration is the only industry in the world that can fail 73 percent of the time and still be profitable."[27] In fact, per year, it costs the US government around $233,600 to incarcerate a youth. In contrast, InsideOUT has taught over three hundred incarcerated minors and adults in southern California for only $2,272 per individual each year.

The staggering difference between these numbers highlights a sliver of the discrepancy of the incarceration system in the US. InsideOUT, although a relatively small nonprofit reaching three juvenile detention centers, has managed to do something incredible that our government has not. Professional writers who work with this program, like Michael Miner, have provided the forgotten individuals with a recognition that has the power to change their lives.

In the first decade of the twenty-first century, Michael joined InsideOUT Writers at the Central Juvenile Hall in Los Angeles. InsideOUT also operates in the Barry J. Nidorf Juvenile Hall in Sylmar and at Los Padrinos Juvenile Hall in Downey. While Michael was training to become an

---

25   InsideOUT Writers. [online] Available at: https://www. insideoutwriters.org/ [Accessed 4 Dec. 2019].

26   Realcostofprisons.org. (n.d.)."The Real Cost of Prisons Project." [online] Available at: http://www.realcostofprisons.org/papers-all. html [Accessed 4 Dec. 2019].

27   InsideOUT Writers. [online] Available at: https://www. insideoutwriters.org/ [Accessed 4 Dec. 2019].

InsideOUT instructor, he observed two different classes consisting of female inmates. Michael commented on this experience. "Generally speaking, I felt as though the female inmates were more mature and expressive with their writing than the males I encountered. However, at the same time, they seemed to hold more obvious grudges that affected their ability to be honest with one another in the classroom."

After his training, Michael volunteered as a creative writing teacher for three hours every Saturday. During his time as a trained volunteer, he only taught young men. He admits that for about the first year and a half of his experience as an InsideOUT writing instructor, he often felt nervous and uncomfortable, not yet aware of how to teach and interact with his students.

In fact, two times when he was teaching, prison guards had to come into his classroom after an alpha male inmate caused him trouble and riled up many of the other juvenile delinquents in the room. "Through every session, however, I began to grow my confidence and eventually gained a certain ability to take control of situations with rowdy inmates," he commented. Whenever Michael felt that one person would inhibit others from learning, he soon felt comfortable kicking that person out of the classroom.

When speaking to Michael about the struggles he endured while participating in this program, he relayed a memory of reading a book that helped him overcome some of his fears and doubts. *Pedagogy of the Oppressed* by Paulo Freire is a book about an aid worker in Rio de Janeiro. The ideologies about the true purpose of aid expressed in this book made Michael reflect upon the effectiveness of his work with the inmates.

What he realized after reading this book and through his own experiences was that aid workers' common downfall is their appeal to false pity. So many people who work for the benefit of others, whether voluntarily or not, often pity those they aim to help. Michael explained how this notion related to him. "I admit that I started my experience with Inside-OUT with this type of mind-set. I constantly believed that I carried the weight of all the students I tried so desperately to break through to. This, however, is a tremendous burden for one to carry."

After reading *Pedagogy of the Oppressed*, however, Michael changed his perspective. His duty wasn't to fix someone but to acknowledge the fact that he was merely there to give his students the tools to fix themselves. This slight change in attitude altered the course of his work with InsideOUT. He felt more in control of situations with inmates. He freed himself of the notion that he was responsible for anything more than providing support in the form of writing and friendship. Through this coping method, he felt much more liberated and confident in his purpose.

I asked Michael to tell me about some of the people he encountered in his years with InsideOUT Writers. The first person he recalled was a young man named Alton. At his time in juvenile detention, Alton was facing up to ten years in men's prison after having been in the back of a car that shot at a cop car. However, Michael began to see Alton as more than an inmate. "I began to see that he was a writer," he stated, "and a great one at that."

Before Alton's adjudication hearing, Michael wrote a letter about Alton's diligence in writing. Michael has written dozens of letters in the past, often delivering three copies to go to the judge, the delinquent himself, and their parents. Ultimately, Alton was released from a sentence in prison. He started a GoFundMe campaign that allowed him to pursue a bachelor's degree at Howard University in Georgia. Michael has met with Alton since his release and is still in awe of the things this boy has been able to accomplish despite his detainment.

"I have seen boys and young men change from functionally illiterate to literate by writing their own stories," Michael relayed. To be functionally illiterate means that they did not have a sufficient ability to read and write to meet daily practical needs, especially in the workforce. By providing the incarcerated youth with this gift of literacy, InsideOUT Writers are giving them the tools to be successful in the outside world if they choose to use them.

Michael stated that the majority of those he worked with opted for writing rap or poetry. He and some other instructors created activities in which the young men would read their own stories out loud in front of their fellow inmates. This was done to address a couple of key problems: the inmates' inability to read confidently out loud and their discomfort with sharing their work. Michael was amazed to truly see the change in those he worked with. "Before the writing session, many of them lacked self-respect. Later through the process, however, I saw many of the inmates grow in self-esteem and self-worth. I watched as they slowly became comfortable sharing their work, sometimes even with their family members, to show them the progress they had been making."

Michael still remembers working with one guy who had been imprisoned for about three months by the time they encountered one another. This young adult had been arrested for excessive meth usage. From this individual, Michael learned how challenging it is for young men to recover from heavy drug usage in the detention centers. Many counties, at least in Los Angeles, do not have any therapeutic measures or medications for those undergoing withdrawals in prison. Michael noticed that the writing sessions held on every Saturday truly helped diminish a bit of the anxiety and depression this particular incarcerated meth addict frequently experienced. This time every week, the inmates actually saw themselves and each other as human beings. It was the only time that they could escape the hawklike watch of the guards and truly allow themselves to breathe and work on their personal improvement and well-being.

According to InsideOUT's web page, the incarcerated youth who participate in the program and eventually get released from detention are encouraged to join their alumni program. In this part of the program, writing circles are held every week to keep the spirit alive and to continue to use writing as an avenue for life improvement. Nationally, the recidivism rate is 75 percent, however, only less than 10 percent of the individuals in InsideOUT's alumni program return to incarceration.[28]

Michael reflected on his eight and a half years as an InsideOUT instructor and explained why he ultimately decided to take a break from this volunteer experience. In fact, by the time I spoke with him, he had not been working with InsideOUT for a little over a year. As rewarding as the work was, he admitted that it had been difficult at times. He explained, "In all honesty, juvenile detention centers are not exactly the most pleasant place to work." Unfortunately, a lot of pain, anger, and sadness is imprinted on the souls of many of those who live and work there.

Although Michael did eventually decide to take a break from volunteering with InsideOUT Writers, when I spoke with

---

28 InsideOUT Writers. [online] Available at: https://www.insideoutwriters.org/ [Accessed 4 Dec. 2019].

him, I noticed something undeniable in the tone of his voice that hinted at the impact this type of work made on his life. As Michael shared his experiences, his laughter indicated an irrefutable sense of admiration for those he worked with. It seemed to triumph over all the stress that came along with other elements of the process he undertook when he had assumed this position.

As I was ending the call with Michael, he thanked me. He expressed his gratitude for stirring up his memories about InsideOUT Writers. Perhaps people like Michael, with booming everyday careers, don't often get as much recognition for the work they do in their free time. When interviewed, the primary questions he is asked must revolve around his foremost career, not the voluntary work he does. He commented after our chat in an email that InsideOUT Writers "was a remarkable experience, and I hope I have the opportunity again to perform that kind of service."

Acknowledging each other for the work we do for the benefit of others is sometimes what inspires us to keep pursuing such work. I hope that all of the Michaels in the world are reignited to get involved with beneficiary work again, even if it is not exactly what they were doing before. Act upon this desire, because this is the work that sparks that internal feeling—the feeling that you are doing something to make the world just a little bit better. This is the work that makes our life something more than purely a complaisant existence. It makes it overflow with purpose and joy.

The intensity of our desire to help others can sometimes be dulled by life's regularity. Sometimes, it is all too easy to let this notion scare you into thinking you cannot do anything to reverse it. It is easy to get upset with yourself when you feel like you are simply wasting time, not doing what you or others feel you are supposed to be doing.

What you have to believe and understand, however, is that deep desires never truly dissipate. Maybe because it's simply who you are, who *we* are. Maybe human beings always have that desire within them, simply waiting to be activated by the power of overwhelming love and compassion.

THE ~~IN~~VISIBLE CYCLISTS

——

David Finklea always made room in his busy schedule for church, despite the amount of work he dealt with in his day job. He prioritized his time spent at Memorial Drive Christian Church because the community had a strong commitment to service that seized him every time he stepped through the doors.

In 2009, David's church in Houston, Texas was organizing a Christmas gift drive for low-income families in their community. One particularly interesting request was from a family for four used but still functioning bikes for children ages six to twelve. At first, David was unsure why this would be the one thing someone requested. Regardless of his initial thoughts, David went home and immediately found his son's first bike that had been hanging unused on his garage ceiling for a few years. He took it down and fixed it up, reminiscing about his family's personal attachment to this bike that had brought his son into the world of bicycling.

David explained, "As I cleaned the bike, I reflected on how happy I was that I hadn't given it away earlier to some faceless charity. Instead, I was cleaning this bike that at one time meant so much to someone I loved, and I was about to give it to someone who otherwise would not be able to afford one." When he got around to calling the church to tell them about his bike donation, there was a very long pause on the other side of the phone. They informed him that someone had already donated $500 to fund the purchase of four bikes and that they had already bought them. Although this was good news to David because it showed the generosity of the people within his community, he was left wondering what more he could do.

Later that day, David decided to call the ministry that his church was partnering with, RaiseUp Families.[29] He notified them that although he was aware that the request for four bikes had already been met, he had another perfectly usable bike that he would like to donate. The ministry agreed that many families would most likely love to have a bike even if they didn't request one. The next day, David crafted an email to forty of his close friends within the community to see if any of them had old bikes of their own lying around.

To his surprise, nearly all forty of these friends responded positively, with a couple following through and bringing used bikes to David's garage. David and his friends thoroughly refurbished the donated bikes, all of which went to families found by the members of the church and RaiseUp.

After the Christmas season, David thought that his work was done. However, in February, he received an unsolicited letter from a family who had received two of the bikes he had refurbished. In the letter, they confessed that without RaiseUp, they would be homeless. It was from RaiseUp that the couple received access to housing and job training that

---

29 RaiseUp Families. "Main Home - RaiseUp Families." [online]
    Available at: https://raiseupfamilies.org/ [Accessed 4 Dec. 2019].

quite literally changed the trajectory of their lives. This letter was signed by *Irma*. David is still not sure if that was the lady's actual name, but from then on, they always thought of this story as Irma's. Irma eventually got a job about four and a half miles from where she and her husband resided.

With her scheduled shifts starting at 5:30 in the morning, Irma had to take two different bus routes, leading her to forty-five minutes of travel time that often caused her to arrive late to work. In her letter, Irma explained that when she received a bike from the ministry, her commute time was reduced by over twenty minutes. This allowed her to sleep in just a bit more, get to her shifts on time and took away all the stress from the often-unpredictable nature of the bus schedules. Now that Irma could make her shifts on time, she knew that she would not be let go, enabling her to adequately provide for her family. This was the first time that David saw the actual impact of the work he and his friends were doing. To transmit this feeling of usefulness that he characterizes as "the impetus for his dedication to service," he forwarded Irma's letter to the forty friends he had reached out to earlier. In response to the email, he received twelve more donated bikes within the week.

Soon David and the others dedicated to this movement saw something really powerful in the making. David found another source of volunteers: high school students. Many students needed volunteer hours for degree programs anyway. Therefore, David opened up volunteer sessions that allowed the youth in the community to learn how to refurbish all of the donated bikes. He held monthly workdays, and anywhere from twenty to thirty student volunteers typically showed up. Many of the volunteers had little to no previous bike-repair knowledge—they didn't even know how to air up a tire.

However, in no time, David and the other senior volunteers taught basic bicycle maintenance skills to these students and watched as they transformed into capable young members of a revolutionary movement.

Eventually, they labeled this initiative as a ministry and came up with the name "Chain Reaction Ministries." They broadened their outreach to other ministries in Oklahoma City, Baton Rouge, and Bentonville. All of these cities have replicated the work of Chain Reaction Ministries with the same mission to provide transportation for low-income families.[30]

As of 2019, Chain Reaction Ministries has put back in service more than eight thousand bikes and recycled more than twenty thousand pounds of metal, all while exhibiting the inextricable link between their faith and the work they do every day. "Many other ministries in the US do similar work," David said, "often focusing on helping people avoid homelessness by providing shelter, basic services, and job training to ultimately allow them to find a stable occupation. But once you have a job, what's the next big challenge? Transportation."

Through his experience, David has found that the gift of a bike can be the difference between individuals keeping their jobs and losing them. David explained that those who acquire the bikes are typically "low-income families, often minorities, riding to and from work in the dark after long hours who too often don't have a voice in government. They are the 'invisible cyclists.'"

In June 2015, a man named James became another memorable invisible cyclist. James came to Houston to build a career

---

30   Chain Reaction Ministries. "Chain Reaction Ministries." [online]
     Available at: https://www.chainreactionbikes.org/ [Accessed 4 Dec. 2019]

in the construction industry. However, James faced a similar issue: the extra stress of taking public transportation in the early morning hours. James had to wake up every morning, hike to get to the bus station, and be there in time to catch the 4:30 bus to arrive at work on time.

The commute exhausted James, but he had no other alternative. He had to make it to work to meet his most basic needs. Therefore, when he caught wind of the work of Chain Reaction Ministries, he sent in a request right away for a refurbished bike. After receiving one, he wrote a testimony for David and the other volunteers. With the help of his bike, his overall morning commute was cut in half. A month after he reached out to the ministry for help, James scored a job doing labor work for Memco Staffing.

The assistance ministries that receive the fixed-up bikes screen their clients to figure out the severity of their transportation needs and ensure that the people with the most desperate needs are met first. Once clients are approved, the volunteers at Chain Reaction Ministries pair them up with an appropriate bike. Chain Reaction Ministries has even had bike recipients ask to volunteer with them so they could pay it forward. "It is beautiful," David added, "to see high school students and folks who are trying to avoid homelessness working alongside one another to fix up these bikes."

I wanted to see what motivated David to keep working with Chain Reaction Ministries and how he was able to balance it while maintaining a full-time job. He said that a lot of his free time in the afternoons and on weekends was put toward the ministry's mission because he has seen the real benefit of what thoughtful, transformational outreach programs can do. His commitment to the mission led him to accept the call to ministry, and in 2013, he became a commissioned minister in the Christian Church (Disciples of Christ).

One of the most rewarding parts of this charity, he said, is getting feedback and words of gratitude from those who receive the refurbished bikes. He commented, "For me, the success of our ministry is not measured by the quantity or quality of the bikes fixed and donated, rather, it is measured by one story at a time. Seeing and hearing about the impact our work has made on individual lives acts as the fuel I need to continue." It only takes one story to prove the benefit of the work.

When individuals think about the needs of low-income communities, efficient transportation may not be the first thing their mind wanders to. Those at Chain Reaction Ministries have recognized this issue without necessarily deeming it to be the direst of these communities' needs. Regardless, they have seen how a lack of such transportation is often a significant overlooked barrier that can be tackled if enough people band together to make it happen.

John Henry Neumann, a Roman Catholic priest in the 1800s, once said, "I have a part in a great work; I am a link in a chain, a bond of connection between persons." Regardless of your religion, race, ethnicity, or place of birth, we can all be a part of this chain: an additional link that contributes to the overall understanding of the interconnectedness of the human race.

THE LITTLE
ORANGE JACKET

———

Three years ago, I encountered a life jacket that would assemble the catapult that launched me into a new perspective. When I first found it in a heap of three hundred other life jackets sent to my school from Lesvos, Greece, an immense ache grew in my chest. This ache was unlike any I had felt before. In fact, I do not know exactly how to put into words the sensation of grief and sorrow that filtered through every avenue of my body when I read the jacket's tag, which said, "Four to ten years old." Adding to the emotions provoked by the size of the jacket itself was what appeared to be a bloodstain.

The moment I held this jacket was the first time *it* truly hit me: the reality of the situation endured by thousands of refugees crossing the Mediterranean Sea. I was holding something that hugged a child who was forced to leave a home that was evidently no longer safe. This tiny vest only saw one section of a child's long, blind journey to *any* place that would one day accept them. The indescribable feeling of that moment falls within the realm of the intensified emotional complexity that overcomes those who recognize their desire to help a situation that they themselves are not directly affected by. This feeling, in my opinion, has the power to turn sympathetic dreamers into agents of change.

The three hundred bright orange vests would soon color the halls of my high school, the American School of Barcelona (ASB). They were part of the first event of a student-led organization I cofounded and ran for the better part of two years called RefugArt.[31] RefugArt, in essence, aims to raise money and awareness for the refugee crisis in the Middle East through events showcasing various forms of art. The heart of the first event was this collection of life jackets—designed by students and staff members to commemorate those who had once worn them. Among these visual reminders of hope for a new life was the tiny life vest that has claimed a permanent frame in my mind's ever-evolving gallery.

These life jackets had been worn by refugees crossing the Mediterranean Sea by boat to Europe as they desperately searched for safer lands. Once we received the life jackets that had been discarded on the shore of Lesvos, the RefugArt team collectively distributed them to ASB students, teachers, staff, and eventually to some parents. The design idea was to treat each jacket with immense respect due to its recent history and the significance it carried. We saw these jackets as haunting visual reminders of the hardships many of their wearers experienced during their journeys to freedom. However, these life jackets also represented strength, courage, and astonishing resilience.

---

31 Instagram.com. *RefugART (@refugart)* • *Instagram photos and videos.* [online] Available at: https://www.instagram.com/refugart/? (https:// www.instagram.com/refugart/?hl=es)hl=es (https://www.instagram. com/refugart/?hl=es) [Accessed 4 Dec. 2019].

Besides designing the life jackets, some friends and I gave presentations in the elementary section of ASB. The purpose of these presentations was to educate future leaders about the refugee crisis and our project. Marta Marcos, Kika De Jong, and I spoke to fifth-grade classes and screened a video posted by the United Nations High Commissioner for Refugees (UNHCR) of a ten-year-old Syrian refugee girl named Niroz. Niroz narrated the short clip, describing her life as a youth in a refugee camp. She showed the camera the hut she lived in and the hole in the ground that was her family's toilet.[32]

The clip ended with a hopeful undertone. Niroz earnestly expressed her aspiration to pursue an education and eventually become a doctor once she was relocated away from the camp. After watching the short video, we gave each of the fifth-grade students a piece of paper and asked them to write down their reflections on how this video made them feel. Most of the students were saddened by Niroz's story and felt a kinship to her, as she was only as old as many of them. Many of the students we spoke to recognized one aspect of the privilege they had been born with and eagerly told us they wanted to help. Some of these same students later went on to design some of the life jackets that were displayed in our exhibition at the end of the year.

My friend Amber Smith and I also spoke to two first grade classes at ASB to deliver a similar message, but through a different, age-appropriate approach. During these presentations, we began by asking the first graders to draw pictures of what they dreamed about. The majority of the kids drew pictures

---

32 UNICEF (2013). "Syrian Children - Refugee Camp Niroz." *UNICEF.* [online] Available at: https://www.youtube.com/watch?v=_IlLwfC2dNc [Accessed 4 Dec. 2019].

of rainbows, their family members all holding hands, smiley faces, and other joyous figures.

After this small activity, we showed the first graders images we got from a saddening yet eye-opening video posted by World Vision.[33] In this video, Syrian refugee children had similarly been asked to draw their dreams. Sadly, the first graders saw how many of these refugee children drew disheartening images, most of which resembled scary and recurring war-induced dreams of losing their homes, friends, and family. Afterward, we had a deeply moving conversation in which many of the ASB children expressed their concern for the dreams of the young Syrian children and wondered what they could do to help.

The comments made by these young students have stuck with me to this day. They reminded me of the goodness and purity we are all brought into this world with. They had not yet experienced true volumes of hate; they only saw rainbows and wanted nothing more than for all other children to see them too.

RefugArt's efforts expanded by passing our idea of the life jacket project on to other schools. Both the International School of Brussels and Leysin American School of Switzerland agreed to join us by creating similar exhibitions with fifty to sixty of the life jackets we shipped to them.

At RefugArt's first-ever event, we displayed the life jackets that had been designed by the ASB community. As one of the leaders, I gave the keynote speech. Additionally, a teacher, our principal, and a member of the Catalan committee of the UNHCR gave speeches. Someone read a powerful poem written by a refugee, first graders sang "We are the World," dancers

---

33 Wvi.org. (n.d.). "Children draw their dreams about Syria." [online] *World Vision*. Available at: https://www.wvi.org/emergencies/video/children-draw-their-dreams-about-syria [Accessed 4 Dec. 2019].

represented refugees' struggle to leave their homes in pursuit of a better life, designers presented a fashion line of clothing made out of pieces of life jackets, and the event held an auction of some of the best student-created life-jacket art pieces. This event resulted in a collection of nearly €4,000, which we donated to the Catalan UNHCR[34] and another astonishing refugee aid organization called the WorldWide Tribe.[35]

After seeing the success of the event that showcased in June 2016, I knew that RefugArt could not end with the school year. The following academic year, Marta Marcos and I created a club to feed off the momentum and enthusiasm built through the success of the last event. On February 16, 2017, the RefugArt team held a shortened movie screening of *Salam Neighbor* by Chris Temple and Zach Ingrasci. *Salam Neighbor* follows Chris and Zach's experience of spending time in the Za'atari refugee camp in Jordan. The two filmmakers went to Za'atari to learn from the families who had fled war and persecution.[36]

In addition to the documentary screening, we organized a panel of refugee crisis experts to answer questions from the audience. Members of this panel included a constituent of the Catalan committee of the UNHCR, Jordi Molina, and a Syrian mother from the ASB community.

I graduated from ASB in June 2017. Since then, RefugArt has continued through the help of other inspired students who still attend the school. They have accomplished more than I could have ever imagined. These students continue to

---

34 Eacnur.org. *ACNUR Comité Español: Sedes y delegaciones.* [online] Available at: https://eacnur.org/es/que-es-acnur/delegaciones [Accessed 4 Dec. 2019].;

35 The Worldwide Tribe. "HOME." *The Worldwide Tribe.* [online] Available at: https://theworldwidetribe.com/ [Accessed 4 Dec. 2019].

36 *Salam Neighbor.* (2015). [film] Directed by C. Temple and Z. Ingrasci.

raise money and donate to organizations like the Worldwide Tribe and the UNHCR. Additionally, they have transformed RefugArt into a means by which students recognize their own ability to tackle social problems. Through RefugArt, many students, myself included, realized that although it is hard to make a difference in our world, we are capable of making a change, even if that change is small.

* * *

When I was fifteen years old, I made the most transformative move of my life from Hudson, Wisconsin, to Barcelona, Spain. In Barcelona, I attended ASB, the school where RefugArt first blossomed.

Attending ASB has been one of the most prominent changes in my life thus far. One day while I looked around at all the people in my cafeteria, it dawned on me how many people from different nationalities sat together and got along. At ASB, we were all constantly exposed to those who were different from us, prompting us to recognize the common links of humanity from a young age. By attending this school, I acquired an indispensable knowledge of the different cultures and traditions of my peers and about myself and how I might fit into the works of the world.

The American School of Barcelona is a private, nonprofit, coeducational international English-language school dedicated to serving students from the greater Barcelona metropolitan area.[37] The majority of the high school students at ASB choose to participate in the International Baccalaureate

---

37 Asbarcelona.com. *American School of Barcelona*. [online] Available at: https://www.asbarcelona.com/ [Accessed 4 Dec. 2019].

Diploma Programme (IB), a degree that gives students the ability to apply to any university in the world.

Like many of my peers, I embarked on the two-year IB journey. One of the unique opportunities provided to me through my high school diploma program was the "Service-Learning Model." The program available to students in high school is called CAS (Creativity, Action, and Service). The ASB service-learning coordinator at the time who was in charge of CAS was Marta Vernet.

Marta has held this position for nearly fourteen years. Her role and responsibilities, although subject to vary every year, revolve around providing meaningful opportunities for her students to give back to their community through acts of service. For as long as I have known her, Marta has done an incredible job in serving as the bridge between the ASB community and external organizations.

Marta helps students keep track of their service work and plays an essential role in motivating each student to actually desire to make tangible changes in their community or elsewhere. Marta was one of the people who supported RefugArt wholeheartedly. Without her, the club would be nothing like it is today.

A variety of amazing service opportunities are available for students to choose from. These opportunities fall into three broad categories: humanitarian, educational and linguistic, and environmental.

In addition to RefugArt, under the humanitarian branch, the ASB economics department has started service-learning trips to Botswana once a year. During this service trip, the students visit the SOS Children's Village and Dukwi Refugee camp. The students also meet with various nonprofits, the local Government's Education and Defense ministries, and the EU and US Embassies in Botswana.

Another international service experience in ASB's CAS program is a medical mission where students travel to a remote town in Peru twice a year to work as translators for a team of American doctors. Throughout the year, the team of students creates and brings marketing and educational materials to post in the rural town's medical clinics. One of the more recent additions to this initiative is to have ASB female students talk to local Peruvian girls about reusable period cups and the importance of attending school. In addition, in 2018, a group of ASB students went to Nepal to aid in building a school and taught English lessons to local children. Alongside these larger projects, ASB students create a myriad of smaller campaign drives, collecting items such as food, cans of beans, Christmas toys, and pet supplies.

Under the branch of educational and linguistic opportunities, a program called Sharing to Learn enables individuals from grades nine and ten to assist English-language teachers with their lessons in local Spanish and Catalan schools. I participated in another program called Bridging through Art where we created artwork with Spanish-speaking adults with mental and physical disabilities at the Fundación Asproseat.[38] Similarly, other students spend their volunteer hours organizing and participating in interactive activities with members of a nearby elderly home.

Another transformative opportunity is through a partnership with the Sant Joan de Déu Hospital. Interested students shadow doctors at this hospital to learn more about the field while they help an assigned doctor practice their English-language speaking. Additionally, Let's VET is a collaboration with a

---

38 Asproseat.org. *Asproseat | Serveis a persones i empreses.* [online] Available at: http://www.asproseat.org/ [Accessed 4 Dec. 2019].

local vocational training school in which ASB students help the vocational students with their English while the vocational students teach them skills in graphic design, cooking, or carpentry.

ASB students also participate in environmental programs such as school-wide recycling initiatives, maintenance at a local park, a yearly beach cleanup, managing a student garden, an environmental club that oversees many of these activities, and more.

I often say that none of these opportunities would be possible without the coordination, motivation, and dedication of Marta Vernet. Her passion for service and providing life-changing opportunities to her students is what makes her so unique and utterly inspirational.

I was not surprised to hear, upon reconnecting with her post-high school, that she has broadened her impact by creating an organization in the little spare time she has. She and her partners, Manolo Garbayo and Jose Sanmartin, have named this organization Win-Win Connection.

Marta explained why she felt compelled to create this organization. "I wanted to transfer all of the passion I had for working with youth empowerment to the corporate world."

In essence, Win-Win Connection designs a variety of service-learning programs and acts as a liaison between the stakeholders. Their three missions are to "connect companies with people, places, and institutions through strategic partnerships and institutional collaborations," transfer "service-learning methodology already consolidated in the international educational field to the corporate world," and to formulate the "communication of good stories that people want to listen to."[39]

---

39   Win-Win Connection. "HOME." [online] *Win-Win Connection*. Available at: https://www.winwinconnection.com/ [Accessed 4 Dec. 2019].

The work Marta does through her programs at ASB and at Win-Win Connection is linked. She further elucidated, "Thanks to these service trips with ASB, I have been able to develop connections in Peru, Botswana, and so on that allow us at Win-Win Connection to replicate similar service trips or missions with other institutions or corporations."

Feeling fortunate to have created a life filled with passion and purpose, Marta reflected, "Not enough talent is being used to solve social and ethical problems in the world. I knew quite early on that I wanted to put my creative and innovative energy into a career path that would be all about creating opportunities for others." And Marta has done just that.

I encountered Marta during one of the most developmental stages of my life, and she looked at me and my peers and not only told us we could make a difference but showed us tangible ways to do so. Any time I had a crazy idea about how to creatively give back to the community, Marta was the first to tell me it wasn't so crazy: it could happen if I elicited the right amount of dedication and compassion to get the job done.

Marta has used her life's work to empower youth and pressure corporations to do their part in benefiting their community. She has so effortlessly shown competence in believing in the capability of others. She is a motivator, a friend, and a true inspiration. Her dedication and belief in others have had mountainous effects on so many. In fact, her empowerment served to transform a little orange jacket into a permanent memory that continues to motivate me, one of the many people blessed to have crossed paths with Ms. Marta Vernet.

EMANCIPATED

———

Caroline Teti grew up seeing poverty all around her. In her birth country, Kenya, the gross national product per capita is around $3,500, whereas this number reaches $59,800 in the United States.[40] As soon as Caroline heard about GiveDirectly, she knew that by joining this organization, she could finally give back to the people of her country in a meaningful way.

GiveDirectly is a nonprofit organization that offers cash assistance to some of the poorest people in the world. Through the use of electronic monitoring and payment technology, GiveDirectly carries out a three-step process to ensure that the donated money is going to the right place and being utilized in the best way possible. To identify which geographics to work in, GiveDirectly uses data available to the public to target poor and remote communities. Then, staff members are sent to these communities as a first step to assess the level and effect of poverty and find recipients for the cash assistance. This is followed by a second and

---

40   Cia.gov. "Africa: Kenya." [online] *The World Factbook - Central Intelligence Agency.* Available at: https://www.cia.gov/library/publications/resources/the-world-factbook/geos/ke.html [Accessed 4 Dec. 2019].

third visit before the recipients are ready to receive their first transfer.[41]

To ensure that the checks are used legitimately, GiveDirectly uses GPS coordinates, crowdsourced labor, and satellite imagery. Those eligible and selected for assistance are given around $1,000 per household, delivered in two tranches of $500. Each recipient is contacted by GiveDirectly's call center after each payment to give an account of how they used the money and any challenges they may have faced. This is done, again, to guarantee that the donations are appropriately deployed.

Caroline is the director of recipient advocacy at GiveDirectly. She leads the organization's fraud prevention work, safeguarding and risk mitigation, content selection testing and dissemination, and provides advisory support to GiveDirectly country offices. For about fifteen years prior to joining GiveDirectly, Caroline contributed to various governmental and nongovernmental organizations in program management and advocacy roles.

Caroline was immediately intrigued by GiveDirectly's mission of giving cash directly to impoverished individuals rather than to partner organizations. She explained, "I wanted to understand more fully what it meant to give people the cash necessary to change their own lives instead of working for an organization who sends members to a community and allocates aid in the way they believe to be best. We must not do this. Rather, we must let the locals decide for themselves."

GiveDirectly stands out from other organizations with similar missions because they are highly technological. "A

---

41   GiveDirectly. "GiveDirectly: Send money to the extreme poor." [online] Available at: https://www.givedirectly.org/ [Accessed 4 Dec. 2019].

lot of our operations are run on digital platforms. This is consistent with the push for a digital economy. There has to be a very thorough understanding of how the technology works among the staff here at GiveDirectly. We also invest in ensuring the transfer delivery platform is always optimal, as this is the core of our work."

GiveDirectly primarily operates in the east African countries of Kenya, Uganda, and Rwanda. By the end of 2019, however, it expanded to other African countries including Malawi, Morocco, the Democratic Republic of Congo, and Liberia. Caroline's primary office is located in Nairobi, Kenya, but she frequently travels to all three operation points within the country, two of which are about six to ten hours by car from her city.

Caroline explained how she sees GiveDirectly's momentous impact through the field visits she conducts. "I have met so many people who have been impacted by the transfers we give, both at a community and individual level," she added.

In fact, many of the individuals that have significantly touched Caroline's heart have been the myriad of single mothers who have received their assistance. "We have had some really intriguing stories about women who have been able to get themselves out of abusive marriages," Caroline highlighted. The money given to these women allowed them the financial capability to leave their destructive husbands. Caroline explained that GiveDirectly has sent cash transfers to many widowed women who have been faced with various social challenges, including land rights conflicts with their families-in-law. GiveDirectly's funds have allowed these women to get through tough times and enabled them "to buy land away from their in-laws." Such an act empowered them and gave them a sense of independence. With the cash assistance, they were able to buy their own land, provide their children with better education, and make other life-altering changes.

According to Caroline, "GiveDirectly launched a unique project in 2016 that tests the impact of universal basic income. In this program, the organization sends monthly, unconditional transfers of $22 each to all adults in selected villages." In fact, as of 2019, the program has benefited over twenty thousand people. Some of these adults receive the money for two years while others will receive it for twelve years, depending on their particular situation. Yet another group of adults receives the equivalent of the two-year support given as a lump sum. GiveDirectly, working with an independent research organization, now provides evidence for the benefits of this type of support on spousal relationships, risk-taking behavior, planning and saving behavior, and aspirations in life.

In many of these rural communities, the responsibility to bring back food and money for the family rests on the husband. When this can't be done, conflict within the household often arises, occasionally resulting in violence toward the women as the husbands get angry that they cannot contribute to the family's livelihood. "So when we introduce both the men and women of households to the transfers, we often see that the women finally feel more included in family affairs and are more empowered to contribute to the livelihoods of their families." According to a study that examined the impact of GiveDirectly's assistance on intimate partner violence, women experienced less physical and verbal domestic violence after a transfer because now both parties were able to contribute financially.

Caroline vividly remembered meeting and working with one woman in Kenya who had absolutely no support from a husband. This woman had broken some of her limbs in an accident. As a result, she had been bedridden for a few weeks. The woman's daughter was left with no choice but to move back in with her mother to help take care of her. When the pair received a transfer from GiveDirectly, their life changed dramatically. With this money, they were able to buy a wheelchair, essentially enabling the woman to become mobile again.

Caroline reflected on seeing this woman the first time she sat in her new wheelchair. "It was beautiful and utterly remarkable. This woman was now able to actually move around her house, go to the bathroom by herself, and get a much-needed change of scenery." With the other portion of the transfer, the woman was able to create a small business to help support herself and her daughter. And she was able to do so within the comfort of her own home in her new decked-out chair.

Caroline, clearly choked up in her reminiscence, commented on the transformative nature of such assistance. "We offer these women economic emancipation . . . for once, they feel free, perhaps for the very first time in their lives."

GiveDirectly's transfers are unconditional, meaning that the recipients are free to choose what to spend it on and do not have to pay it back. "Once we hand out a transfer, we give the individual the opportunity to decide how they can use it to change their life," Caroline elaborated.

GiveDirectly believes that if aid organizations dictate how communities should use the funding, they are limiting their own ability to address everyone's unique problem or situation. Caroline and the others at GiveDirectly are changing this narrative by providing cash transfers: an act of empowerment that leads to the renewal of dignity for the vulnerable.

AN UNFORESEEABLE EFFECT

One of my favorite soccer coaches when I was growing up in Hudson, Wisconsin, was Allie Knutson. Although I was young when I knew Allie, the memories I associated with her name were always positive. She was my favorite coach because she was a young woman whose soccer skills encouraged me to elevate my own. I remember telling my mom I wanted to be like Allie when I was older: a strong woman who could do anything men could do or better.

I hadn't spoken to Allie since the days I lived in Wisconsin, but when my mom informed me that she was in Belize with the Peace Corps, I decided to reach out to her to see if she could tell me more about her experience and those affected by her work.

The Peace Corps offers opportunities in many remote communities around the world for motivated US citizens to immerse themselves in a foreign culture and work alongside local leaders to address the direst needs of the people within their elected community. Among others, the principal overarching objectives of the Peace Corps are to "help the people of interested countries in meeting their need for trained men and women," "to help promote a better understanding of Americans on the part of the peoples served," and "to help promote a better understanding of other peoples on the part of Americans."[42]

When I first reached out to Allie, she began our conversation by informing me she has worked with the Peace Corps twice. In 2009, Allie packed up her life and embarked on her first experience to a small village in Mongolia. There, Allie went through three months of training before settling into a lead teaching position at a local school.

Allie was the first American ever to live in the Mongolian village where she was stationed. "Everything I did, the people in the community would observe and often try to imitate," she explained. At one point during her stay, Allie created a soccer club with the kids in the village. "I remember all the kids being shocked that I would play with them because in their world, girls didn't play sports. Not only was I a woman, but I was also their teacher." Allie would play with the kids during recesses and would occasionally organize tournaments after their classes ended. Allie broke the gender stereotypes that hinder the native girls' opportunities to participate in "boy" activities. Just through the simple act of playing with the children as a woman, she was able to show the community that girls could be just as capable.

Allie would often help some of her students in after-school tutoring sessions if they were falling behind. Many of the students in this village would not go to school due to a myriad

---

42 Peacecorps.gov. "Work for the World." [online] Available at: https://www.peacecorps.gov/ [Accessed 4 Dec. 2019].

of reasons. Allie soon learned that a lot of factors come into play when an impoverished child decides whether or not to go to school that day. For example, if the child did not get breakfast in the morning due to their family's inability to purchase food, they most likely will not be able to go to school because they will be unable to concentrate. Allie explained how, unfortunately, "many of these unexplained factors often get overlooked when considering the situation from an American perspective where punctuality is everything."

It was difficult for Allie to talk about the impact her work may or may not have made on the community she lived with in Mongolia. Allie admitted that although she could often use the spotlight on her every move as leverage in having her opinions heard, it could be extremely frustrating as well. She felt as though all eyes were on her, waiting for her to make the tangible changes she too wished she could see right away.

Allie knew that what she was doing made a difference, but she struggled with self-doubt when some of the changes were not as easily identifiable as she may have hoped.

"After every school year," she said, "I would always reflect and wonder if I really did much to help, you know, and how much we actually accomplished. So that can be challenging, not always being able to see your impact up front."

Regardless, Allie's unshakable belief in the power of education pushed her to keep believing in her own added value in the community. By showing the children she cared about them and the quality of their futures, she had no choice but to have faith that they felt valuable and empowered in return.

Allie worked in this town for two years. When she returned to her life in the United States, she became a schoolteacher for the subsequent seven years. "When I got back to life in the US," she said, "I started to truly see how much we as a society take things for granted. Those in Mongolia had nothing but still found more happiness in the small, everyday things." Eventually, Allie readjusted to life in the US. In 2018, however, she explained, "I felt antsy again, like I needed to be somewhere I wasn't."

In reaction to the fire under her feet, Allie applied to Peace Corps Response in Corozal, Belize. Peace Corps Response is a ten-month program that sends professionals or Peace Corps veterans like Allie to work on projects in the most desperate need of assistance and expertise.[43] When in Belize, Allie's role shifted from a traditional English schoolteacher to a literacy specialist.

This job was much more specialized than the position Allie held in Mongolia. When she and the other veteran Peace Corps volunteers first arrived in Belize, they trained for a few weeks in the capital city, Belmopan. After the training, Allie moved to the northern district of Corozal. Once there as a literacy specialist, she became responsible for coaching eleven Belizean standard one (second grade) teachers how to enhance their teaching skills for the benefit of their students. The primary objective of Allie's project was for each of the teachers' struggling students, which in most schools was at least half or most of the students in the class, to receive fifteen minutes of targeted literacy interventions per day. The teachers she worked with were from eight different schools in Corozal. Allie hoped her coaching would generate a sustainable change in the Belizean education system.

A student at one of the schools Allie worked with struggled a lot in his classes. This little boy's particular teacher was

---

43 Peacecorps.gov. "Peace Corps Response." [online] Available at: https://www.peacecorps.gov/volunteer/is-peace-corps-right-for-me/peace-corps-response/ [Accessed 4 Dec. 2019].

really strict and, as Belize has different norms for teacher-student relationships, the teacher would often yell at this boy when he wasn't excelling as well as she supposed he should be. The boy would take a long time to get simple tasks done efficiently and without error, like copying down the heading to his papers. He had a short attention span and was often scolded for talking to others and playing with little toys he would bring from home. Allie noticed this little boy's behavior when she came to the class and started to talk about him with his teacher during break times. She soon found out that the little boy's home life was very difficult.

Although Allie didn't work directly with the students all the time, as her primary job was to observe and coach the Belizean teachers, she made an effort to spend more time with this little boy. As a result, he started to warm up to her more and more. In the spring, Allie would pull this boy and others who struggled with reading and writing aside to do some individual testing. The next time Allie came into the school a few weeks later, the boy ran straight up to her and hugged her for a long time. Seeing the growth in comfort this boy and others had around her gave her a sense of assurance that her work mattered. Allie helped this boy without scolding him. She helped him see his capability by just spending a little extra time with him, convincing him through actions that he was worth it.

Another of Allie's roles in Belize was to ensure that the teachers conducted a comprehensive reading screening of the students every semester. She would assist the teachers if they had any trouble and helped them look at the data and figure out which students needed more guidance and attention. The year that Allie was there was the first time that every second-grade teacher was expected to implement such a screening. During the screening of one of Allie's teachers, she noticed a boy who was being particularly disruptive, so she decided to stand next to him. "He wasn't really paying attention or following along. When I would try to redirect him, he would tell me he thought the test was easy because he was the oldest of his peers because he had to repeat the class," she noted. Even though the boy was explaining how easy it was for him, he was getting most of the screening questions wrong.

In response to the boy's unimpressive screening results, he had to be in his teacher's intervention group all year long. Allie commented on this teacher. "She was an absolute rock star; her teaching style was excellent, and she had several reading intervention groups throughout the year. So it was no surprise that her intervention students' reading and writing improved dramatically from the beginning of the year to the end." Allie saw how the boy's behavior improved so much after every intervention. When she assessed him again in March, he was ecstatic to read for her and show her all that he could do. In the fall, the boy had read a thirty-word passage in about five minutes. In the spring, he read that very same passage in less than a minute, exhibiting extreme progress.

Allie saw other students who previously didn't know the sounds of letters starting to read entire sentences. She heard stories about students who didn't use "to like coming to school," but were "now loving the school year and the 'games' they got to play during intervention time." She had students who wanted to show her what they could read during their breaks and after school. "They became so proud of what they could now do thanks to their teachers' dedication."

Allie spoke highly of not only the students she met but also the teachers she coached. "The teachers I worked with were excited. And I could never help but get very excited too, because when we saw students improve, it made everyone want to work even harder."

Empowering individuals to make the changes they need for themselves rather than doing everything for them is immensely important. If the latter approach is employed, communities develop a certain reliance on foreigners. This can be very destructive when the foreigners they depend on leave their mission. Allie's program, the Peace Corps Response, aimed to alleviate this dependency and create a sustainable educational practice through empowerment and coaching.

* * *

As an undergraduate student in the nineties, Wendy Smith studied both anthropology and philosophy. She immediately gravitated toward philosophy because she found herself always contemplating philosophical questions. As she puts it, "A lot of epistemological, metaphysical, and moral questions that you ask in philosophy really cause you to reflect on life, and this way of thinking can truly broaden your perceptions." Eventually, she realized she wanted to couple her philosophy studies with anthropology because she enjoyed finding the overlaps in the role of culture and poverty and how they define the human existence or knowledge.

"I think my studies as an undergraduate student led me to be really curious about why the world is the way it is," Wendy reflected.

During her undergraduate studies, she also participated in an exchange program at St. Lawrence University in Kenya. There, she lived with five different Kenyan host families. While studying abroad, Wendy met a myriad of Peace Corps volunteers who also lived in the area. Through these interactions, she understood for the first time that working on social development projects could actually be a lifelong vocation. From these associations, the idea of joining the Peace Corps first entered her thoughts.

Right after she graduated, Wendy immediately applied to the Peace Corps, not quite sure if it was going to work out, but she figured she might as well give it a go. After a year and a half of waiting, she got accepted. However, when she did, the position she was offered was as an agroforester in Benin, a small country in Western Africa bordering Togo and Nigeria. The fact that she was put in this position, working with agriculture, was ironic in her eyes because she had no experience in the field. She always laughed about it, assuming whoever assigned her to the position must have thought she'd have some useful knowledge to apply to the assignment since she was born and raised in Wisconsin.

Before Wendy was sent off to Benin, she went through three months of training to prepare her with some simple ideas and approaches she could later implement in her assigned village. When she arrived in the small Beninese village, she realized she would be virtually alone in her duties. The governor was supposed to be working side by side with her, but unfortunately, that wasn't really the case. "When I first got to the village, I was to be living in for the next two or so years," she stated, "I was left to figure out what my value to this community would be. I questioned myself and my assets, thinking, *What did I really know?*" With this self-reflection, Wendy decided she primarily desired to focus on community organization.

"I think the Peace Corps is honestly the deepest and most formative experience for many who participate in it. You really have to learn about how change happens and how to identify the large challenges in a community. You are working hand in hand with the people in the community, searching for effective ways to make sustainable changes." The Peace Corps doesn't give you a big budget or a vehicle. Instead, you must simply figure it out and do the best you can do with the limited resources you have. "It's really about looking at ways to solve community issues and seeing how you can play a role in being the organizer and the one who empowers others in the community to continue the work long after you are gone," she added.

Even though Wendy's designated sector was agriculture because she spoke English, many local teachers would ask her to come into school classrooms on occasion to speak to the children. As she was increasingly asked to speak at the schools, she decided to use the opportunity to focus on environmental education. With this, she began working toward mobilizing the young people in school by showing them how they could be actors for social change around the environment.

Wendy also did a lot of work with a women's group in her community while still focusing on their environmental impact. She worked with local women to create dry-season gardening habits with the aim of improving child nutrition. She also worked on an initiative that trained women on how to use credit to create their own small businesses.

One of Wendy's primary goals was to familiarize these women with the ins and outs of animal husbandry so they could have their own cows. "In the part of the world where I was volunteering, women would often have to work on their husbands' farm fields, which would grant them less time to work on establishing their own financial means," Wendy delineated. Besides training the women, Wendy also acted as a liaison between them and nonprofit organizations in the area. "So I guess you could say not only was I a community organizer; I was also their connector and cheerleader."

Wendy's initiatives radically helped women engulfed in the Beninese culture for a myriad of reasons. For one, women don't have a lot of say in most Beninese societies. "Looking back at it now, people were probably laughing from a distance, thinking, 'Whatever, let this white girl do what she needs to do for a year or two,'" Wendy laughed. "But in reality, it really changed those women's lives."

There were a lot of tensions between ethnic groups in the area where Wendy lived. One day, when she was still living in Benin, lightning struck the village fields. Tragically, two children died. When deaths like this happen, the local people process their grief through either a traditional way or a mystic tradition that some may consider to be similar to witchcraft. One of the ethnic groups that believe in more mystical happenings consulted with healers and religious leaders.

They ultimately determined that the boys' deaths had been a punishment for having wronged a man of the opposite ethnic group who claimed they had stolen money from him. "I never really believed this to be true," Wendy said. "I think it might be a way for people to try to make sense of senseless losses—but nevertheless, it caused a lot of unprecedented tension." Conflict stirred between individuals who believed the man and those who believed in the innocence of the two deceased boys and the genuine erratic essence of their death.

By the time this conflict arose, Wendy had established herself as a sort of undeclared leader and someone many in the village looked up to for guidance. As a result, Wendy found herself in the middle of this odd and abstract debate. "I ended up working with two local leaders, trying to facilitate these conversations to ease tensions. It's funny when I think about it now because I really had no legitimacy in that position." Wendy explained that as a Peace Corps volunteer, she became part of the fabric of the community but was never a true member, which allowed people to trust her unbiased perspective.

In addition, she wasn't bound by the cultural constructs of many other locals. For example, many other women in the community would have been immediately overlooked if they had spoken up. However, since Wendy was an "outsider," people oddly looked up to her. "As a foreigner, particularly in a very small and rural community, you have this opportunity to engage people to chat about stereotypes and open up new conversations about the way things are done and by whom."

Using her position of anomalous power, Wendy tried to intervene in ways that benefited the less influential members of the community, especially the children. If a student couldn't make it to an exam because they lacked access to transportation or a girl got pregnant and was convinced she couldn't go back to school, Wendy explained that she would try to go in and talk to them—essentially doing what she could to encourage them to pursue their life plans against all odds.

Wendy ended up extending her stay in Benin from two years to three. Wendy made this change because "it takes a while to truly understand the problems in the place you are sent with the Peace Corps. Simply figuring it all out is almost a yearlong process. And then, by the second year, you can finally get into doing what you are really meant to do. I personally extended my stay for a year because I wanted to continue to solidify the work I had been building throughout the two previous years."

After her third year, Wendy went home to pursue higher education. "The Peace Corps was very much the foundation from which I then decided to apply to graduate schools to deepen and pursue my interests. I chose to focus even more on international development throughout my higher education." Wendy decided to attend the Teachers College of Columbia University in New York for graduate school. As soon as she graduated, she secured a job at the International Rescue Committee (IRC) and was one of the first people to work on truly refining the international organization's approaches for education in emergency situations.[44] At the IRC, Wendy focused a lot on addressing the question of how, as an organization, they could meet the educational needs of refugees and displaced children.

Throughout her few years working at the IRC, Wendy was able to travel around the world, working with a lot of different communities who were trying to meet their educational needs despite the harshest and most difficult of circumstances. After she left the IRC, she went on to work for a myriad of other nonprofits, her position always seeming to revolve around education and the promotion of worldwide literacy. Some other organizations she worked for include World Vision[45] and Worldreader.[46]

For years after she left Benin, Wendy kept in touch with the community she had spent three years helping and befriending. In Benin, she had lived with a family that consisted of a father, his four wives, and their fourteen children.

44 Rescue.org. [online] Available at: https://www.rescue.org/ [Accessed 4 Dec. 2019].

45 World Vision. "Give a future full of choices." [online] Available at: https://www.worldvision.org/ [Accessed 4 Dec. 2019].

46 Worldreader. "Creating A World Where Everyone Can Be A Reader." [online] *Worldreader.* Available at: https://www.worldreader.org/ [Accessed 4 Dec. 2019].

She became incredibly close to nearly every member of this large yet eminently welcoming family. A year after Wendy left, she heard from one of the family members that John, the father of the family, contracted a disease and died a few months later. "When I found out, I was devastated. I was mostly heartbroken for the kids because I knew what would most likely happen to them," she alluded.

Culturally, in this community, the wives of the deceased husband would be sent back to their home communities, often without their children. Instead of accompanying their respective mother, the children would be distributed among their father's brothers. "I remember being so afraid that if I didn't go back and intervene on some level, the kids would become orphaned. I worried about this because many of John's brothers were not as well off financially as he had been. Not only this, but I wasn't sure they had the emotional or social tools at their disposal to really educate these fourteen children."

In response to the burning need within her to see the success of these children she had grown to love, Wendy went back and ran what she likes to think of as a nearly "twenty-year social experiment." She traveled back to the small village in Benin to negotiate with John's brothers and convince them to allow all the children to stay together in the house John had built for the entire family before he died. Wendy eventually found one of the brothers to be in a decent enough headspace to be able to live with all fourteen children while distributing financial responsibility evenly between all of the other brothers. This brother also ultimately agreed to grant each of the mothers of the children regular visitation rights.

Wendy informed the family that she herself would support the schooling for all the children. "And so my husband, Francois, and I made this commitment to support the tuition costs of these children. We continued to do this for around fifteen to twenty years. Our payback was that we got to see fourteen beautiful people grow up to be educated, empowered adults." In fact, one of the boys Wendy and her husband supported is now living and attending a college in Georgia, finishing out the American educational experience he had always dreamed of obtaining. "It just goes to show that you never know the long-term effects your service will have," Wendy smiled.

Through all of Wendy's years chasing after what she felt like she was meant to do, her approach to life in general shifted catastrophically when her three children entered the world. She expanded, "When I was younger, and before I had my own family, I was really driven by inner social change and the desire to be a part of programs that brought about meaningful results like the Peace Corps. I think that as you get a little bit older and you have kids, success becomes about being a part of and maintaining a social mission but not letting it get too demanding that you ignore personal relationships and your local community."

Wendy's experience and the magnitude of her impact caused me to reflect on Allie's words and the hesitation she had with affirming whether her work made a huge difference in her students' and teachers' lives. Wendy's experience in the Peace Corps was over more than twenty years ago while Allie's was more recent. A lot of the projects and assignments of the Peace Corps yield wonderful results, many of which may seem small at a glance yet life changing when compounded over many years.

Wendy spoke to this notion. "That's the thing about the Peace Corps. I think many of its volunteers don't go back often enough to be able to see the long-term effects of their services. Because if they did, they would have no doubt their work hadn't been for nothing." Who knows, maybe that small, previously inattentive boy who grew comfortable enough to hug Allie every time he saw her developed a sense of confidence that propelled him toward an opportunistic future he would have never grappled with otherwise.

Most people who embark on an experience similar to the Peace Corps are bound to face similar doubts, but peace of mind can be found in understanding that there is an undeniable and often unforeseeable potential that lays beneath the surface of anything we think we know. Service and passion to help others will never go unnoticed. It all makes a difference, no matter how minuscule it looks at first glance.

THE BIONIC KIDS

———

Every year, approximately five out of every ten thousand children are born with congenital limb reductions. These defects affect many aspects of a child's life. Possible ramifications include slower development of motor skills, necessitated external assistance, mobile limitations, and perhaps the most jarring of all, emotional and/or social difficulties that arise with an abnormality in physical appearance.[47] However, children have the potential to overcome these challenges, often through the help of prosthetics.

The effects of these differences and potential accessibility solutions rarely crossed Albert Manero's mind until one day while he was sitting in traffic on his way to his university's lab.

"I was listening to the radio," Albert recalled. Ivan Owen, the inventor of the first 3-D printed mechanical hands, was being interviewed on a radio talk show. Albert rushed into his research lab that very same day and told his classmates

---

47   Centers for Disease Control and Prevention. (n.d.). "Facts about Upper and Lower Limb Reduction Defects | CDC." [online] Available at: https://www.cdc.gov/ncbddd/birthdefects/ul-limbreductiondefects. html [Accessed 4 Dec. 2019].

he needed to use their 3-D printer for an idea that had come rushing to the forefront of his mind.

Albert, now finished with his PhD in mechanical engineering from the University of Central Florida (UCF), had always known he wanted to use his multiple engineering degrees to make a difference in individual lives. At the time, he just had not yet found out how to make this a reality.

When Albert first finished his undergraduate studies, he was confronted with the decision every college student has to face: which path to follow. Right after he obtained his bachelor's degree, Albert was accepted to continue his research and decided to pursue the route of graduate education because he was extremely passionate about the work he was able to do.

As he continued with his research, he worked tirelessly in a UCF lab with other motivated students. He loved the technology side of what he was learning and realized that something was continuously burning underneath the surface of the incredible work he was doing. He seemed, somehow, to be waiting for a wave of inspiration to kindle this flame.

Who knew his day stuck in traffic would soon assume the form of this wave?

"I saw an opportunity to leverage what I was learning and researching in a different way to support a child's dream," he explained. After a local family reached out to ask if he and his team could design a prosthetic arm for their son, Albert and his fellow researchers rallied together. No more than eight weeks later, in July 2014, Albert created his first prosthetic arm for this little boy, Alex.

"When Alex got his prosthetic arm—I still remember the moment he was able to hug his mom for the first time with two arms. In this moment, the rest of the team and I all teared up and really felt the reason why we had to continue with this work. We realized we wanted to help many kids have these moments," Albert said.

After the successful fit of Alex's new prosthetic, or "bionic," arm, as Albert likes to call it, the mission to create more arms expanded and led to the establishment of Limbitless Solutions. Spearheaded by Albert and now housed at UCF, Limbitless uses electromyographic (EMG) technology to create bionic arms for children with accessibility limitations. This nonprofit focuses primarily on the creation of arms that are functional, cost-efficient, and personal.

Limbitless's website says, "Since our arms are 3-D printed with ABS plastic, we produce them at a much lower cost than other prosthetics in the medical market." With the lower cost of production, Limbitless is able to raise funds to cover the remaining expenses, leaving the "bionic kids" and their families with little to no cost for the entire process of clinical trials and their final product.[48]

Limbitless prides itself on the ease and function of their arms. In fact, they focus on ensuring that each arm is light, accessible, and mobile to express various gestures and hand movements.

Alex, the first child they helped and an avid superheroes fan, asked Albert and his team if his arm could be designed like the arm of his favorite superhero, Iron Man. This request was the first that set Albert and his team on a mission not only to create functioning and affordable prosthetics, but also to allow the kids to express themselves and be proud of the arm they would carry with them. After working with Alex,

48   Limbitless-solutions.org. "Learn All About Our Bionic Arms | Our Work" [online] *Limbitless Solutions*. Available at: https://limbitless-solutions.org/ourWork [Accessed 4 Dec. 2019].

Albert conveyed that "interactions like these make you realize, 'Wow, this could really be powerful for so many people.'"

Alex met Robert Downey Jr., who collaborated with Limbitless and helped spread the word of their efforts through a video with Alex that is shared on the organization's web page. Robert plays the lead role of Iron Man in the *Iron Man*, *Avengers*, and *Spider-Man* movie series. Capitalizing on his character's bionic suit, Robert visited Alex after he received his new arm that mirrored that of Iron Man's. The two bonded over their cool, out-of-this-world arms.[49]

Until meeting Limbitless Solutions, ten-year-old Anni had no right forearm due to a birth defect. One day, Anni was taken to an aquarium to meet the star of *Dolphin Tale*, her all-time favorite movie. Winter, the starring dolphin in this film, swims with a prosthetic tail after having lost her real one.

"She really inspires me a lot," said Anni of Winter. "I love her movie. They told me I was going to feed her fish, so when they opened the cooler and I saw this, I'm like, 'This is not fish. What am I looking at?'"

In the cooler where she expected to see a fish, she saw a new prosthetic arm. *Her* new arm designed by Limbitless.[50]

Albert professed, "Anni is a ball of joy. My heart was just melting when she went up and hugged me and she didn't want to let go. That definitely choked me up, too."

To reflect her interests, Albert and the rest of the team at Limbitless Solutions created a prosthetic arm for Anni that

---

49 Youtube.com. (2015). "The Collective Project: Robert Downey Jr. Delivers a Real Bionic Arm." [online] *Limbitless Solutions*. Available at: https://www.youtube.com/watch?v=oEx5lmbCKtY [Accessed 4 Dec. 2019].

50 Youtube.com. (2015). "Winter the Dolphin helps deliver Anni's New Arm." [online] *Limbitless Solutions*. Available at: https://www.youtube.com/watch?v=5PNJEsn2Pgk [Accessed 4 Dec. 2019].

was covered in a Hawaiian flower design. Anni commented on what having this arm has done for her. "I can wear it outside and a lot of people will stare at me and they won't be like 'what is that?' They'll be like, 'Oh my gosh, it's so pretty' or 'Where'd you get it and where can I get one?'"[51]

Another member of Limbitless's bionic family is a little girl named Julianna. Julianna, born without a left arm, received a UCF-branded prosthetic arm and got to cheer alongside the UCF cheerleading squad. Through this experience, Julianna became friends with the cheer squad she always looked up to, gained a new easily accessible bionic arm, and inspired the team and people all over the nation with her persistence, joy, and positivity.[52]

These arms gave Julianna, Anni, Alex, and many other children the ability to evince their personalities and converted some of the shame or sadness they may have had into a newfound sense of pride and source of elation.

As of October 2019, Limbitless has expanded its outreach to two other exciting innovations. Project Xavier uses a technological model that allows immobile persons to move their wheelchair without their hands. EMG sensors are placed on the individuals' temporalis muscles, allowing them to regain a sense of mobility through a simple flex of the jaw. When the sensors pick up on a movement of the jaw, the wheelchair's joystick activates.

Although this is a relatively new realm for Limbitless, its potential is perpetual. By providing immobile individuals

---

51 Youtube.com. (2018). "Limbitless Solutions." [online] Available at: www.youtube.com/watch?v=43sFzm_a4cQ [Accessed 4 Dec. 2019].

52 Youtube.com. (2015). "Julianna's Limbitless Opportunity With UCF." [online] *Limbitless Solutions.* Available at: https://www.youtube.com/watch?v=5PNJEsn2Pgk [Accessed 4 Dec. 2019].

the chance to reclaim mobility with technology, Limbitless is giving an insanely beautiful gift. It makes their clients feel like they have some power again.

Another way Limbitless has expanded in recent years is through a video game training initiative. Utilizing the same EMG-powered technology from their bionic arms and mobility sensors, the team at Limbitless has created video games and accessibility controllers for new bionic kids. The idea of these games is to aid bionic kids in getting used to their new arms and learning to use them in a fun and engaging way.

According to Limbitless's website, their current mission is to "raise enough funds to donate a hundred bionic arms (at $1,000 per bionic arm for hardware) and fully support a hundred bionic kids (at $10,000 per bionic kid) in future clinical trials." As of October 2019, Limbitless has created arms for the first eighteen bionic kids and supported them through their ongoing clinical trials.

Despite the progress they are making, they cannot reach their goal without the belief in their work. Simultaneously, they cannot help these children without many individuals working together to make a difference and see it through.

When asked about what these arms mean to the kids, Albert responded that if you were to ask the kids themselves, they would most likely explain that it was never about simply using both hands. Instead, those at Limbitless understand what is much more important is that the bionic kids discover the courage and ability to express themselves.

"When the kids smile as they see how well their new arm fits, it brings us all to a moment that replays in our heads anytime we need motivation for what we do," Albert said with a smile.

Being born without a limb many of us take for granted is so far out of our imagination. How often do you think about the function of your upper or lower arm? How many times a day do you appreciate the mobility of your hand or fingers? For bionic kids, this feature of their reality is out of their control yet can potentially be altered. We can help them reclaim what has been missing: a sense of ownership and the confidence to tackle the challenges thrown their way.

A THIRST FOR MORE

In 2008, 1.1 billion people around the world did not have access to safe, clean drinking water.[53] Seth Maxwell first heard this statistic from a photojournalist friend when he was only nineteen years old while he attended the American Academy of Dramatic Arts. Seth was shocked to hear that so many people struggled with something that he had never once questioned his ability to access.

After hearing this statistic, Seth could not stop thinking about the global water crisis and began to research it. He found out that people all over the world were walking miles to fetch water out of rivers, ponds, and swamps and contracting preventable waterborne diseases in the process. According to the Centers for Disease Control and Prevention (CDC), "unsafe drinking water, inadequate availability of water for hygiene, and lack of access to sanitation together contribute to about 88 percent of deaths from diarrheal diseases."[54]

---

53   Thirst Project. "World's Largest Youth Water Organization." [online] Available at: https://www.thirstproject.org/ [Accessed 6 Dec. 2019].

54   Cdc.gov. "Global WASH Fast Facts | Global Water, Sanitation and Hygiene." [online] *Healthy Water | CDC*. Available at: https://www.cdc.gov/healthywater/global/wash_statistics.html [Accessed 6 Dec. 2019].

Compelled by these astonishing facts and figures on water inaccessibility, Seth began talking about the issue with some of his friends from college. Soon after, Seth and seven of his closest friends decided to establish a club at their school aimed at raising awareness about the issue. From this club, Seth explained, "We began to create events around Los Angeles to get people to talk about the issue, raise awareness, and take action."

One of the largest events Seth's club set up was on March 22, 2007, on World Water Day. He and his group took to the streets of Hollywood and gave away free bottles of water to engage anyone they encountered in a conversation about the global water crisis. They asked people if they were aware of what was happening and prompted them with questions to identify potential donors. In one day, this college club was able to turn the $70 they spent on the bottles of water into nearly $1,700: a colossal sum of donations that was later used to fund the creation of their first freshwater well.

After this day, some of the people they met on the streets began calling them. A few asked Seth and the others if they would be willing to go to their school to speak about the global water crisis to try to band people together who would be interested in starting up similar clubs on their campuses. Seth said with a laugh, "When this was all happening, after we had gotten several similar requests, we thought, 'What? We are just eight college kids. We have finals next week!'"

Due to their mounting requests, the group organized several school speaking events from which various fundraising efforts were made. Before Seth had much time to process the impact of their speeches, they received checks totaling about $12,000. From these donations, Seth and his friends realized there was a tremendous untapped potential in students and other individuals their age around this issue. From this realization, in May 2008, they created the organization that is still up and running today, Thirst Project.

Thirst Project, with the support of young people throughout the nation, aims to "end the global water crisis by building freshwater wells in developing communities that need safe, clean drinking water."[55]

To continue executing and supporting water projects around the world, Thirst Project needs funds. They are constantly in need of more resources to expand their impact. All of Thirst Project's ventures are on the ground; they do not fund third-party nonprofits.

Throughout the years, this organization has worked in five countries. However, the country in which they have made the largest impact is Eswatini, formerly known as Swaziland. On April 19, 2019, King Mswati III changed the name of the country to Eswatini in honor of the country's fiftieth anniversary of independence from the United Kingdom.[56]

Seth had a myriad of reasons for considering Eswatini when he and his team were debating where to dedicate most of their initial efforts. "For one, the country is small, only about 1.4 million people. The idea that we were potentially able to give the entire country safe water was incredibly attractive," Seth admitted.

As they focused their efforts in this country, they soon found out that as of 2017, "more than one-quarter of the adult

55 "Our Mission," Thirst Project, accessed December 10, 2019, https://www.thirstproject.org/about/our-mission/.

56 Cia.gov. "The World Factbook: Whats New." [online] *The World Factbook - Central Intelligence Agency*. Available at: https://www.cia.gov/library/publications/the-world-factbook/docs/print_whatsnew.html [Accessed 6 Dec. 2019].

population was infected by HIV/AIDS" and the country "has the world's highest HIV prevalence rate, a financial strain and source of economic instability."[57] Seth soon realized that the relationship between water and HIV was extremely critical. He noted that in rural communities, even if individuals have access to great medical treatments and antiretrovirals, if they still drink from contaminated water sources, they are very prone to catching diseases.

Therefore, unfortunately, the water they drink has a higher likelihood of killing them faster than their HIV/AIDS. Seth elaborated, "The ability to make a positive impact on two issues at once is really another one of the main factors that led us to identify Eswatini as our country of focus." In fact, Thirst Project currently builds more projects in Eswatini than any other stakeholder.

Seth's personal role in the organization as the chief executive officer involves overseeing a lot of the fundraising efforts. The team travels around middle schools, high schools, and college campuses to get the youth motivated to do their part in diminishing the severity and breach of the global water crisis.

In addition to his role in raising funds, Seth also enjoys participating in many of the organization's groundwork projects. The four countries other than Eswatini that Thirst Project currently operates in are India, Uganda, El Salvador, and Kenya. In each of the field operations in these countries, full-time project staffers oversee the activity in their homeland on the ground.

Seth recalls meeting one of these native employees, Sibu, at Thirst Project's initial scouting and data-collecting trip in

---

57 Cia.gov. (2019). "Africa: Eswatini." [online] *The World Factbook - Central Intelligence Agency.* Available at: https://www.cia.gov/library/publications/the-world-factbook/geos/print_wz.html [Accessed 6 Dec. 2019].

Eswatini. At the time, Sibu was working for the branch of government that houses the water affairs department. Sibu was assigned to drive Seth and his team around as they were collecting data. Seth got to know Sibu quite well over this month-and-a-half assignment.

Near the end of the trip, one evening, Sibu asked Seth if it was okay if he was a little bit late to pick them up the next day. Seth replied that of course it was okay and asked if anything was wrong. Sibu confessed that he needed to take his daughter to the hospital because she had been having bad diarrhea and was sprouting other symptoms of someone who had drunk contaminated water. Upon hearing this upsetting news, Seth was confused, because he had assumed Sibu was from the city where there was safe drinking water. Sibu told him that he lived in a rural village just outside the city. Seth was shocked because Sibu had been driving them around to nearly seventy-five different communities that did not have access to safe drinking water and never once mentioned that his own village was one of them. Upon hearing about the lack of clean water in Sibu's village, Seth made sure that it became Thirst Project's next target area.

In August 2010, Seth met another local who inspired him to push forward with the mission of Thirst Project. At the time of their encounter, Juliet took care of eight children in her community, none who were her own. All of the children had lost their parents to AIDS. Juliet herself had also lost her husband and two of her own children to the disease. Before Thirst Project constructed a water program in her village, Juliet and the other women used to have to walk about half a football field to a nearby stream to fetch water. This stream was, sickeningly enough, the same water source that animals and people would often defecate in.

After hearing how contaminated water contributed to the devastating losses of many of Juliet's loved ones, Seth and his team decided to implement a project in her community that eventually provided clean and safe drinking water. Seth smiled. "Juliet was so excited by the fact that the children in her community would not have to experience the chance of disease from drinking contaminated water like she and others her age did."

As of 2019, Thirst Project has provided over 330,000 people worldwide with access to clean and safe drinking water. Through their tours to 1,100 campuses in the US, they have motivated over 2.5 million students to become involved by donating or spreading awareness of the crisis. All the funds raised from schools around the country have totaled up to over $9 million, all of which have directly contributed to their water projects.

I asked Seth what motivated him to continue working with Thirst Project and not return to the life he had previously envisioned for himself. He responded without hesitation, "I believe the access to clean water is a human right."

He went on to explain that waterborne diseases kill more people every year than HIV and malaria combined. The reason why he decided to get into social impact work may not have been derived from the same long-settled desire that I had since I was a child. Instead, Seth's involvement developed into a passion like Chris Temple's did: it began with an aha moment. He explained, "It was much more driven by the issue itself, and it occurred to me that I simply could not do nothing about it."

Instead of being consumed by the idea that everything he does needs to be widely significant, Seth has narrowed his focus to making a difference on an individual level. "If every person I encounter leaves feeling loved," he expressed, "that is success."

Seth also commented on the emotional toll of his work and admitted that looking at how huge the waterborne illness issue still is can sometimes be dispiriting. However, whenever his mind turns to this thought pattern, he has learned how to quickly reset it. "I really try to focus on the positive impact of what we are able to do because if not, it would be way too easy to get overwhelmed by what is wrong in the world. And in my opinion, that is simply not productive. So rather than focusing on the negative, I focus on what we can do to make change."

It can be extremely difficult to not let the severity of an issue discourage you from persevering. However, by honing in on the mass changes you and others are capable of generating, and the *people* whose lives you have the ability to improve, the gravity of the task that still lies ahead will seem less daunting. You will always have hills to climb, but do not let that trick you into believing that life is more thrilling when sitting motionless at the bottom. Take that leap. Gear up for the climb.

TO INSPIRE ONESELF

———

Megan Ultimo was with her abuser from the age of sixteen for about thirteen years. At the time, however, she wasn't even truly aware of what was happening to her and never categorized it as abuse until 2014—when the worst of the worst happened to her.

Megan was bruised from head to toe by her abuser, aware that she could have very easily lost her life. Back in 2007, she had been diagnosed with multiple sclerosis. During this violent incident seven years later, Megan was slammed to the ground by her husband so hard that her back cracked. Megan still remembers waking up the next morning aching from the physical and emotional pain and realizing that she *had* to do something to change her situation. She started to do research to properly educate herself on domestic violence and ways to navigate a life away from it.

Soon after her near-death experience, Megan made a thirty-second Flipagram that she later posted online for the world to see. The first fifteen seconds of the video showed all of her bruises, and the second half was of her and her two little girls. The video in its entirety showed the worst and the best outcomes of her damaging marriage. To Megan, the purpose of this video was to exhibit herself and her daughters as examples of how you can be happy after overcoming something as traumatic and scarring as domestic violence.

Kristen Faith, the founder of Break the Silence Against Domestic Violence (BTSADV), encountered Megan's Flipagram on the internet and immediately reached out to her. Kristen asked Megan if she wanted to come to a sisterhood retreat that she was organizing for survivors of domestic violence. Megan ultimately agreed and flew out to San Diego where Kristen resided at the time.

When Megan joined the retreat, fifty other "sisters" joined her. Being around other survivors empowered Megan and made her feel way less alone in her thoughts and feelings. To this day, BTSADV hosts a survivor sister retreat in the first half of every year to allow more women to find consolation in others who have gone through similar unspeakable circumstances. In essence, this retreat aims to "empower female survivors of domestic violence as they partake in workshops devoted to promoting a positive self-image, individual development, life skills training, and enrichment courses."[58]

After the retreat, Megan felt inspired to participate in BTSADV's mission of providing community resources and support to individuals affected by domestic violence. She answered messages and phone calls of those in need of guidance and an open heart. Soon enough, she began to permanently volunteer with the organization. Her first responsibilities with BTSADV were to answer Facebook messages and to post advocacy campaigns on their social media sites. She soon realized, however, that what she wanted more

---

58   BTSADV. "Survivor Sister Retreat" [online] *Break the Silence Against Domestic Violence*. Available at: https://breakthesilencedv.org/retreat [Accessed 4 Dec. 2019].

than anything was to get more involved by speaking directly to the individuals in need of support or advice. In late 2016, Megan was trained to do just this. She began to answer calls on their help-lines, the main form of communication between clients and BTSADV volunteers.

At the time, only Megan and one other person were in charge of answering phone calls while Kristen continued to manage the organization as a whole. Since Megan joined, the organization has grown immensely. In fact, as of today, BTSADV has help-line advocates on call almost every single day. Volunteers are located all over the country, most often answering calls and emails from the comfort of their own homes. Now, Megan continues to answer desperate emails and phone calls from those seeking help and manages the entire team of volunteers to make sure that someone will always be available to assist.

Now that Megan coordinates volunteer help-line advocates, when she has an opening for a position, she conducts phone interviews to ensure that the most empathetic and compassionate individuals are selected. Once accepted, Megan holds trainings where she explains in detail what the help-line entails and what is to be expected of BTSADV volunteers. All of the current help-line volunteers, like Megan, are domestic violence survivors who have great insights and advice to offer their clients. Other volunteers are relatives or close friends of those who have endured domestic violence. Essentially, Megan ensures that all of her potential volunteers are prepared for any and all questions that may come their way.

Although the work BTSADV advocators do helps people in desperate situations, it is without a doubt very trying work. When I asked Megan about the greatest struggle she has endured while answering calls or emails, she responded,

"The triggers that come along with it." She went on to explain how certain conversations with individuals can bring up past memories with her own abuser. These triggers, of course, can make the job very emotionally draining. She articulated, "Another difficulty that comes with a job as trying as this is the gravity of the decisions people ask me to make for them."

Megan has had a myriad of calls from individuals pleading for answers. For example, she has had plenty of people ask if they should go to the sheriff's station immediately to report their abuses: a decision that is extremely hefty and has the unforeseeable ability to either truly help or hurt the client. What Megan has learned through all of these tough conversations, however, is that she has to remain calm, strong, and supportive. She considers herself a deeply empathetic person and therefore truly puts herself in her clients' shoes to aid them to the best of her ability.

Megan receives the reassurance that her efforts are truly making a difference every day. Most of her clients respond to her help and support with sincere words of gratitude that fuel her desire to keep working. She also has had many clients who call on a consistent basis over a long period of time. From this type of caller-receiver relationship, "you see the transformation of your clients in their words. It is often different from the first time that you talked to them. You can hear the impact you've had on them in their voice."

Megan recalled one lady that she spoke to very frequently for a few weeks. During their conversations, the woman was enduring a court hearing that she had initiated to accuse her husband of domestic abuse. The lady was going through a lot and simply appreciated having Megan there to listen to her and validate her feelings. "She always asked, 'Is this a normal feeling?' And almost all the time, my response was 'Yes, it is normal to feel this way,' which I think definitely made her feel understood and less alone." Megan felt so much for this lady she didn't even personally know. So much so that she ultimately decided to take after-hours calls from her: the only time this lady could temporarily escape the responsibilities of the court hearing.

One of the first calls Megan ever received was from a man who was being abused by his wife. BTSADV volunteers don't get many calls from men, but when they do, they are always so proud that the man found it within himself to seek help, overcoming the societal embarrassment that men often feel when their masculinity is threatened. This particular man wanted help but kept repeating that he didn't want to lose his wife. He simply wanted her to change her outbursts and abusive behavior. Part of this plea most likely stemmed from the fact that he had kids with his wife and that he was frightened that he would lose them if he reported his wife to authorities.

The man spoke with Megan weekly for about a month. Although Megan cannot ensure that the individuals she speaks with actually follow through with her advice, she knows that her work is valuable. She explained that "a lot of people like this man just want to vent and have somebody who will listen to them." Megan has become that person for so many.

When I asked Megan what motivated her to continue with this line of work, she replied, "I am innately a helper. Someone needs to do this type of work, so who better than somebody who has lived through it themselves?"

As terrible as Megan's abuse was, she firmly believes that her experience needs to be heard. She explained how sometimes people can't seem to comprehend situations like domestic abuse if they have not personally been affected by it. Many don't understand why the abused party doesn't just leave. By hearing stories like Megan's, it is so apparent that there are many more layers to the issue. She proudly stated, "If just one person can hear my story and be educated about the red flags of domestic violence, then it's all worth it. Everything is worth it."

After speaking with Megan about her experiences with BTSADV, I was interested to know who inspires her. Her response shocked me with its ravishing honesty. "I don't know if this is an answer that a lot of people would give," she said, "but I would say that I inspire myself every day. I inspire myself because, after going through what I've been through, I am still able to rise above it all." I couldn't agree more with her statement, and I believe that responses like this should become normalized. Recognizing the beauty in ourselves enables us to be inspired by our own actions. This is a unique type of insight that propels further self-growth and effort toward helping others with what we have learned through our own lived experiences.

Every minute in the United States, approximately twenty people are physically abused by their intimate partner. In fact, according to the National Coalition Against Domestic Violence (NCADV), one in seven women and one in twenty-five men have experienced this type of violence.[59] I believe it is important to take into account that anyone, regardless of gender, can be a survivor or a perpetrator. As a culture, we often understand sexual, emotional, and/or domestic violence as problems that solely impact women. This, however, does

---

59   Ncadv.org. "National Coalition Against Domestic Violence." [online] NCADV. Available at: https://ncadv.org/statistics [Accessed 4 Dec. 2019].

not create a lot of space for men to heal or acknowledge the trauma that male survivors have experienced. In fact, the lack of recognition of male survivors limits our understanding of the complexity and intersectionality of these forms of abuse.

However, according to these statistics by NCADV, cis men do disproportionally enact domestic violence. Therefore, we can infer that, more often than not, domestic violence is born from the phenomenon of toxic masculinity. The idea that masculinity inherently equates to dominance has, unfortunately, infiltrated the woodwork of most societies in the world. The damage this concept creates is not only particularly adverse for victims of domestic violence but for girls and women in general. It solicits a discomfort and a fear of unwanted things happening to one's body that is sometimes impossible to suppress.

Many females develop this undeniable sense of instinctual wariness toward men from a very young age. The feelings provoked within girls and women from situations of male-inserted dominance are not discussed enough. It's not simply the act of being taken advantage of that stings. It's the feeling of discomfort, dread, and dehumanization that carries on long after the doing is done.

This feeling of consternation that many females have, although not always activated, will most likely forever be swimming somewhere deep within unless something drastically and systematically changes during our lifetime. Through every experience of trepidation, it is hard not to build up a wall and distance ourselves from the people and things that remind us of it.

I have seen others and even myself do just this . . . until more stories like Megan's were told. I am absolutely horrified by how many people have endured both domestic and sexual violence, asymmetrically affecting those on the margins of their societies. However, through others' use of storytelling as an avenue for advocacy, I have seen how universal these feelings and experiences truly are. Hearing these stories has begun to morph the shame I used to feel from countless unpleasant encounters with boys and men into something entirely new: it has lit a fire within me. And Megan and I and so many others are not only ready to talk about it, we are ready to change it.

A BRIDGE OF HOPE

———

In 2017, the Pew Research Center estimated that 10.5 million people were living in the United States without documentation.[60] According to Steve Larson, accredited doctor and founder of the nonprofit clinic Puentes de Salud, this population has the lowest probability of receiving adequate health care.

Historically, undocumented immigrants were generally ineligible to receive Medicaid, thus prohibiting these individuals from obtaining federal subsidies for private insurance. However, under the federal Affordable Care Act that was enacted in 2010, such migrants are no longer required to have insurance to receive care under Medicaid. If these individuals have low incomes and meet other criteria, they are legally eligible to receive health care, but only in some places throughout the US through free and charitable clinics.

Nevertheless, Steve pointed out that there is still a lot of injustice present in the US health care system today. For example, the World Health Organization (WHO) has a policy

---

60 Pew Research Center. "5 facts about illegal immigration in the US," [online] Available at: https://www.pewresearch.org/fact-tank/2019/06/12/5-facts-about-illegal-immigration-in-the-u-s/ [Accessed 6 Dec. 2019].

on prenatal care. Prenatal care, in this policy, is declared a universal human right. However, unfortunately, this "universal right" is not implemented here in some of our very own states, as most undocumented immigrants do not have access to such resources.[61]

On February 6, 2018, I attended a film screening of the documentary *Clínica de Migrantes*. In essence, this film highlighted the story of a volunteer-run hospital clinic cofounded by Steve Larson called Puentes de Salud in the city of Philadelphia. At this clinic, 99 percent of patients are undocumented immigrants living below the poverty line. The inspiring documentary follows the stories of a few of the patients and the workers at the clinic. Steve actually attended the event itself, adding to the entire effect of the documentary, as he was able to make side commentary about the scenes in the film.[62]

Steve Larson is half Swedish and half Puerto Rican. Through an interesting set of circumstances, Steve's father and mother met in New York City and married in the late fifties, an era that had a tremendous amount of prejudice toward people of color.

Steve and his family grew up in a very anglicized community in southern New Jersey. "In fact, we were the only Puerto Rican family I knew of," Steve added. Despite the fact that both of his parents spoke Spanish, they had not taught him and his siblings the language because they wanted them to blend in among the other kids at their school. Steve

61 Who.int. (2012). *WHO's Respectful Maternity Care: The Universal Rights of Childbearing.* [online] Available at: https://www.who.int/ woman_child_accountability/ierg/reports/2012_01S_Respectful_ Maternity_Care_Charter_The_Universal_Rights_of_Childbearing_ Women.pdf [Accessed 7 Dec. 2019].

62 *Clinica de Migrantes.* (2016). [film] Directed by M. Pozdorovkin.

explained that this was what a lot of Hispanic parents decided to do during this time. "This way," he said, children had "less chance of running into prejudice and racism."

After years of schooling to become a licensed doctor, Steve realized he wanted to learn more about the diversity of the world outside the US. "I took some time to travel and realize the beauty of the world, how big it is, and that our similarities should define us, not our differences. All around the world, mothers worry about their babies, grandparents worry about their grandchildren, and they all worry about food on the table. Those are the things that make us human."

Through his travels, Steve considered ways he could connect his desire to break down barriers faced by disadvantaged populations and his life back home in Philadelphia. "You can go places in our hemisphere and get experiences that fuel your passion. For me, that was Central America. There, I glimpsed the reality of the world. Before, while immersed in academia, you live in isolation, somewhat of an ivory tower. So trying to reconnect with all that really brought me to Guatemala, Nicaragua, El Salvador, and other places was difficult, but it taught me more than I could have ever guessed."

After Steve took time to travel, he went back to the US for medical school. When he graduated, he found the prospect of global health to be sustaining, as it satisfied both his desire to make use of his degree and to travel internationally. He soon after realized that he could practice and refine his skills while connecting with the communities in southeastern Pennsylvania that are in the shadows of his institution.

Beginning in 1992, for years, Steve went back and forth once a week between Philadelphia and Kendall Square, an area where many undocumented individuals reside. "From my years of traveling, exploring, studying, and learning, I realized that I wanted to build some sort of free clinic to meet the needs of the undocumented community. However, I realized that if I wanted to ever build anything, it had to be from the bottom up. It couldn't be cut down. From this notion, I decided to build a free clinic involving the priorities and values specific to the undocumented community."

When conceptualizing a model for the clinic, however, Steve faced a couple of realities. "Number one, nothing in this world is free. Everything has a cost." Therefore, as he soon unearthed, the notion of building a free clinic as he envisioned was simply not a long-term, sustainable project, as it was bound to leave little option for growth. "By giving free screens for blood pressure and small checkups, you are still not providing any sort of adequate follow-up to any of the problems you have uncovered. So my model couldn't be a free clinic. The model would not focus on basic health care because, ultimately, health care is utterly expensive." Instead, Steve and his cofounder Dr. Jack Ludmir understood that their model had to include education and investment in the long-term wellness of their patients.

Steve attributed his decision to some of the lessons he learned from the impoverished communities he visited in places like Nicaragua and Guatemala. "For example, the problem of diarrheal illnesses in developing countries kills two million children a year. A short-term solution could be to give antibiotics to a diarrhea-ridden community. However, antibiotics will only cure their diarrhea for about a week or two. If you don't go to the extreme and change the actual environment in which they are living, they are just going to end up sick again. Metaphorically speaking, you've got to go up the river to fix the problem. So if you go upriver, you're going to literally clean the water and ensure proper sanitation.

It is also about teaching the communities about these values to actually make an impact on their health."

When first grappling with Puentes's mission, Steve deduced that they would have to tackle the short-term problems first by meeting the immediate needs of their clients. Steve extended this idea. "We needed to stop the bleeding, so to speak. To do that, we had to be able to provide health care with the consciousness that health and wellness is often determined by socioeconomic status." After they had the short-term needs of the population they were working with under control, they could then start to think about the long-term solutions to their problems, such as the establishment of expansive and educative health programs.

As a result, Puentes de Salud was established in 2003 but did not achieve nonprofit status until 2009. Throughout the years, this clinic has treated patients that had absolutely nowhere else to go and currently treats around 6,500 undocumented people per year who, as a result of the situation they were often born into, had not been able to receive health care in a traditional manner.[63]

To tackle long-term problems, Puentes de Salud expanded its outreach to education. For a target audience of children ranging from ages three to eighteen, a branch of Puentes called Puentes Hacia el Futuro (PHF) provides additional assistance for Latinx communities in the Philadelphia area. Their programs currently include early childhood development, an after-school mentoring program, the Lanzando Líderes adolescent program, and a summer literacy camp.

---

63   Puentes de Salud. (2019). "Puentes de Salud-Nonprofit-Health-Wellness-Latino Immigrant-Philadelphia." [online] Available at: http://www.puentesdesalud.org/ [Accessed 7 Dec. 2019].

In addition, Puentes established adult education programs such as English as a Second Language and Financial Literacy (ESOL). To get the community involved, for the last ten years, Puentes has recruited and trained over five hundred collegiate students to join them in serving underserved Latinx communities through both clinical care and the educational programs for adults and children.

The film *Clínica de Migrantes* followed the story of various immigrants who received help from the volunteers at Puentes de Salud. One such story was of a pregnant woman who came in to see Dr. Jack Ludmir with her mother. Dr. Ludmir, the cofounder and director of its women's health services, was worried that the mother of this pregnant woman was not supportive of her daughter. He suspected this upon examining the daughter's arms, which were covered in bruises.

When the doctor asked the mother what had happened, she responded, "I burned her by accident," with no expression. After speaking with the young woman privately, Dr. Ludmir discovered that she had a history of suicidal thoughts and actions. From this conversation, Dr. Ludmir was able to give the young woman the help she needed despite her unwilling mother and her lack of documentation.

In recent years, the number of immigrants attending Puentes de Salud has grown to new heights. Therefore, the clinic has been trying to increase its funding. Steve explained how one of the hardest parts of this work is when they are simply unable to do it because they do not have the resources, either the money or the insurance, that would enable them to get the proper diagnostic studies. One way the board of Puentes addressed the lack of funding was by asking for financial assistance from local restaurants where many of their patients were employed.

Some of the restaurant owners agreed to donate, but others, even though they employed the undocumented, thought it would simply be easier to turn a blind eye to this specific population and problem. Consequently, throughout the years, clinics like Puentes have had to accept the fact that they will most likely only be sustained through sympathetic agents and voluntary action.

A huge reason for the success of Puentes de Salud has been its community health educators. Community members step in to assume many of these voluntary roles at the clinic with the simple intent of helping where they can. These volunteers take the lead in training the Latinx communities in Philadelphia about diabetes, nutrition, obesity, and much more. A lot of Puentes's patients work fifty to sixty hours a week, and free time is a luxury for them. When you tell them simple health tips such as, "you need to exercise," it sometimes seems unfathomable to them because when they do receive any time off from their strenuous job, they need to relax to take care of their mental state. Understanding this truth, the community health educators have tried to develop training programs that are interactive and upbeat despite the jarring issues they discuss.

Steve, as the executive director, is in charge of a lot of the leadership duties at Puentes de Salud. Although he is only at the clinic itself one night a week, with this position, he has been able to witness and hear about the impact Puentes makes on a daily basis. "When you are dealing with people who are living in poverty and who are virtually invisible in this country, every time you encounter them, it is a victory. The fear that we can dismantle and the reassurance we can provide really makes every encounter enriching," he commented.

Puentes has gotten national recognition after their stories and hopes for the future of their organization was released in the documentary. Steve is so thankful for the opportunities *Clínica de Migrantes* has curated for the mission of Puentes de Salud. "The beauty of going around the country and talking about the documentary is that many of the audience members have been part of community organizations, all at very different stages of growth. I have often found groups of concerned citizens who hear about us and genuinely want to do something about it," he expressed. They, as well as the patients Puentes works with, give him hope that the pursuit to eradicate the injustice in our health care system is a battle worth fighting.

It is disheartening to think of everything that migrants have experienced even prior to their struggles to integrate and be accepted in the United States. Something as simple as adequate health care cannot be received in the country these migrants have always idealized and dreamed of being welcomed into. The majority of these people sacrificed everything to get into the country. Crossing through Mexico, the way the majority of Puentes's patients enter the US, is extremely dangerous. Unfortunately, many of those who attempt to make this journey cross-country do not make it very far. Before entering the US, many migrants face immense problems with drug cartels, corrupt police officers, kidnappings, human trafficking, sexual slavery, and more.

By educating citizens and promoting an awareness of what many undocumented migrants have endured, perhaps people will open their eyes to the humanitarian issue we have a very tangible way of dealing with thanks to clinics and organizations like Puentes de Salud. Steve Larson believes that more clinics that take in the uninsured must be established throughout the US.

According to many scholars such as labor economist Ethan Lewis, immigration has been proven to boost the US economy, despite the belief of many that immigrants are taking jobs from Americans. In an interview with Steve Inskeep from NPR, Lewis adds, "There are very few Americans with which they [immigrants] compete. They often do jobs at the lowest rungs of the economic ladder."[64] They are not the leeches of our economy, as some ruthlessly view them to be without considering their humanity. They, more often than not, contribute where they can and simply aspire to live in a place that is safer and more economically prosperous than their home country.

The lack of health care for the undocumented is not a political matter, it is a humanitarian one.

64 Npr.org. (2018). *NPR Choice page.* [online] Available at: https://www.npr.org/2018/10/24/660112915/immigrations-impact-on-u-s-jobs [Accessed 7 Dec. 2019].

A MARKET OF
THEIR OWN

———

Esra Ozturk was ten minutes away from the airport in Istanbul, Turkey, on the day of a terrorist attack. On June 29, 2016, forty-five innocent civilians were killed in this airport while more than two hundred individuals were severely injured. Esra was supposed to fly that night but had changed her flight last minute for trivial reasons. She watched the news in horror as chaos erupted throughout the airport; people were crying from both physical and emotional pain, running around to escape or in a desperate attempt to find their loved ones.

At the time, Esra was only eighteen years old. She was returning to Turkey from the United States, where she had been going to college. She intended to visit some family members during her summer holiday. While back in Turkey after the terrorist attack, however, her trip back home turned into something much more. She soon began to see the significant damage the airport incident had made on the country's previously renowned tourism industry.

Many tourists that the Turkish economy relied on so heavily were now terrified to enter the country in fear of another malicious attack. The majority of those who worked in the tourism industry as entrepreneurs were uneducated women whose entire livelihoods depended on selling their products at touristy marketplaces. As this industry declined and a lot of flights were refunded, many of these women were left with no way to provide for themselves and their families.

Observing all that was happening to the women of her country of origin, Esra traveled to southern Turkey. On July 10, 2016, she met a woman, Iknur Celikdilk, at a local market where she was selling her own handcrafted jewelry. Esra spoke with Iknur and soon found out how the recent decline in tourism was affecting her livelihood. Esra immediately expressed interest in what Iknur had to say, thus allowing the woman to feel comfortable confiding in her.

Iknur explained to Esra how her current state of desperation was not simply a product of the attack but also a result of various unfortunate circumstances that had occurred in her personal life. She confessed that, in just three years, she had lost all of the important men in her life. Iknur lost her husband and her job simultaneously. "I was left with nothing. I had no money, and I was scared of what the next day would bring. That is when I started to work with my hands. I entered this business to give myself therapy and ended up making some money."

Iknur also lost her father to cancer shortly after the death of her husband. A few years later, she lost her thirty-three-year-old son. After all of these tragic losses, Iknur felt adrift and confused. She didn't know how to navigate an existence without three of the most salient men in her life. As a way to cope with her pain, she devoted her entire efforts to the work of jewelry making.

Iknur now believes all of her hard work has not only paid off, but it has saved her life. She expressed, "Each person I make happy with my work keeps me going. This is my everything. My bread, my health, my relief, my love, my hope." After speaking with Iknur and seeing the passion and devotion she had for her work, Esra knew she had to do something to help Iknur and others like her succeed in such an unpredictable market.

For nearly two years after the day they met, Iknur introduced Esra to other working women like her in the community. Through these interactions, Esra created valuable and meaningful connections. The following fall, Esra returned to the US and sold the women's jewelry to her college friends. As she got the hang of selling, Esra created a web page to maximize her outreach. More women were continuously added to the partnership with the help of Esra's family members that lived permanently in Turkey. They went out and searched for more female street workers in need of assistance.

As this initiative grew, it soon transformed into a company. Arzo became a social enterprise because its business model allowed them to use the money earned to put back into their business and pay for new materials for the Turkish women to make more products. Although categorized as a company, Esra was adamant about not letting the overall mission become all about transactions and profits like a normal business tends to develop into. The women Arzo worked with needed consistency and stability. In the two years this business was up and running, Arzo gave the female workers valuable feedback on how consumers were responding to their products and ultimately helped them get back on their feet.

Essentially, Arzo staff members worked to bridge the gap between female Turkish artisans and the US online market. Arzo members were responsible for advertising the handmade jewelry of Turkish women on their website and finding partner stores that agreed to sell their products. "I just wanted to help women, especially those who didn't have institutions of support or educational opportunities to fall back on," Esra disclosed.

As Esra's website developed, product presentation became a high priority. To personalize the products, the story of the woman who made the piece of jewelry was always posted next to its image. Esra viewed this initiative as a way to spread awareness for the struggles these women faced and the ways they overcame their barriers. These stories, Esra said, shed light on the humanistic side of what may otherwise be inaccurately portrayed on the news.

She explained, "I think the news sometimes skews reality and disconnects us from other human beings because of politics, religion, race, or just physical distance. Instead, with these products, I wanted to show how people who have been through such ugly, hard times can use their pain to create something beautiful."

By attributing each product to a story, Esra hoped that each consumer would feel more connected to the person who made it even though they had never met. She added, "This is really important in social work: the ability to make people feel as though we are all dealing with similar feelings in this human experience."

Esra chose the name *Arzo* because it is a word of Middle Eastern origin. She explained, "Different people spell it in different ways, but I just picked my version of the spelling. It means 'hope' and is often a name given to baby girls born in difficult conditions." She identified her business with this meaning because it was created to instill hope in women who were facing trying obstacles.

Esra also prioritized personal relationships with Arzo's entrepreneurs, a factor that most definitely helped the women feel less alone and fearful during their recovery journey. One of the most appealing aspects of Arzo's model of operation, in my opinion, was their mission of giving desperate women the means to support themselves.

Esra spoke to the accredited nature of their work. "I think it's important to realize that most people can solve their own problems if you empower them to." By focusing on empowerment rather than a pure donation, the Turkish women were able to learn valuable skills that had the power to perpetuate a more sustainable future.

One of the women that made products for Arzo was named Sevcan. Sevcan lived in Bozcaada, Turkey and worked hard every day and night making handmade products such as anklets, bracelets, and head scarves. Sevcan told Esra that her main source of motivation to keep working as hard as she did was the dream of being able to put both her son and her daughter through school. Sevcan put an immense amount of work into each piece she created. She once told Esra, "I make everything with love. That is the only way I can handle everything I have to do as a mother and a worker." Through Arzo's help in selling her products online, Sevcan eventually succeeded in providing her two children with life-changing education.

Unfortunately, Arzo only lasted two years. When I asked Esra the principal reasoning behind Arzo's discontinuation, she admitted that the business model was simply not strong enough to withstand the political turmoil in Turkey at the

time. For example, product regulations they had not anticipated soon made it inefficient and financially strenuous to
send the products to the US.

Esra had initially established Arzo as a start-up and therefore did not have all of the benefits and ease of operating
oversea shipments that massive corporations tend to have.
Esra herself was only a sophomore in college when the entire
enterprise began and had a lot of other life responsibilities on
her plate. Regardless, Esra knew her work held undeniable
value. "When I first created Arzo, I did so with the pure
intent of helping as many women as I could. This enterprise
wasn't made to become a huge machine. That simply wasn't
the goal," she reflected.

One of the first things Esra asked me during our interview
was if her story would still be relevant even though Arzo was
no longer up and running. I immediately told her that the
longevity of the initiative is not what mattered to me, nor
should it to anyone. After speaking with her and hearing
her story, I saw that the work Arzo did was incredible while
it lasted and impacted so many women's lives. Even if it had
only influenced one woman's life trajectory, it would still have
been noteworthy. I was also remarkably inspired by the fact
that Esra was only just out of high school when she started
up this entire movement.

Esra felt compelled to change a tragic situation that she
was not directly affected by. She was motivated by her compassion and sympathy and used it to transform the lives of
women whose senses of hope had been dismantled along
with their industry. She provided them a reason to continue
to create, smile, and love. She gave them a reason to live.

YOUR GREATEST POWER

———

Certain people open up your heart with the warmth of their voice, exuding sincerity with every word they speak.

Without even knowing Aimee Halfpenny, the first time we spoke, I could immediately sense she was one of these people. The way she talked about others, those she worked with and those she worked for, was lathered in undeniable layers of kindness and appreciation. She spoke with a kind of knowing. Her voice sounded seasoned, hinting at the notion that she had experienced many personal struggles with working in a field almost begging for burnout, yet had known a triumphant collection of times in which she managed to overcome them. Aimee has undoubtedly been through a lot, yet she still speaks fondly of her past, is optimistic about her future, and cares deeply about her present.

From a young age, Aimee understood suffering and the idea that bad things happen to good people. She commented, "I have always been extremely empathetic. Ever since I was little, I remember feeling very deeply for others, already understanding the sense of walking in others' shoes." When she attended college, she focused her studies on psychology, hoping to one day help others in the way she and her family were supported. Growing up, Aimee's family and friends helped her navigate life with a brother who battled addiction issues.

While in college, Aimee attended a seminar that discussed the ins and outs of fundraising. At the end of the seminar, she spoke with some of the attendees and ended up unexpectedly securing an events job with a nonprofit in Orange County, California. At the time, she was only twenty-one years old. This first job paved the road for the discovery of her love for meaningful nonprofit work.

Later in her life, Aimee worked for a community-driven organization called Mama's Kitchen, and its mission resonated with her the most. In 1990, Mama's Kitchen was founded by a caregiver in San Diego who gathered volunteers to prepare and hand-deliver cooked meals to the doors of individuals who were suffering from AIDS. The mission expanded in 2004 when a food pantry was created to give low-income, HIV-positive San Diego County residents access to free groceries. Since the organization's initiation, Mama's volunteers have prepared and delivered three free meals every day to those struggling with HIV/AIDS and their families. In 2006, the individuals who are eligible to receive such deliveries expanded to those battling cancer.[65]

Aimee started working at Mama's Kitchen as an events coordinator and grant writer. "I kind of grew up professionally there. But it also really embodied everything I love about that type of work and what I have chosen to do with my life," she added. At Mama's Kitchen, their mission is in action when they deliver meals to people who are critically ill. She elaborated, "It takes an army of people to make it happen.

---

65   Mamaskitchen.org. "Mama's Kitchen | Nourishing the Heart, One Meal at a Time." [online] *Mama's Kitchen*. Available at: https://www.mamaskitchen.org/ [Accessed 4 Dec. 2019].

People cook food and package it, then you have this army of delivery volunteers who come in three times a week to take food all over San Diego County. It is huge." Within six months of working as an events coordinator and grant writer, Aimee got promoted to director of development. With this new position, her role included overseeing all the grant writing, event planning, and development strategies: a position she held for nearly seven and a half years.

As a paid employee, Aimee was especially impressed by the dedication and generosity of their volunteer staff. "These incredible people donated their time, even though the majority of them have other full-time jobs. They just did this on the side because it gave them meaning and it was the right thing to do. And it mattered." Aimee expressed, "It changed me . . . getting to be a part of it. To see what a group of caring people could do when they came together was so fulfilling."

When the volunteers couldn't show up for some reason, Aimee would often go out and deliver the food herself. She stated, "When you deliver the meals, you see people in their skin and bones. They often don't have resources and are plagued with hospital bills . . . so the dignity that comes with receiving a warm meal is irreplaccable."

What she noticed through her various outings was that a lot of their clients with breast cancer were single moms. In fact, it wasn't uncommon to deliver to a single mom with four or more kids in the home Occasionally, the children of these moms would tell Aimee they didn't want to bother their moms by asking them to cook because they knew how much they were struggling. "It was heartbreaking, the fact that they felt guilty to ask to have their needs met," Aimee said.

Although Aimee was touched by nearly every person she delivered food to, one particular little boy stuck out to her in her years with Mama's Kitchen. The little boy had a severe form of cancer, leaving his mother no choice but to quit her job to support her son. The father had to drastically reduce his work hours as well, "because when you have a very sick child and their siblings at home, it is a lot to manage. You basically need one person managing the sick child full-time, and then on top of regular work, you need someone to help manage the stress of school and life of the other siblings." On top of having cancer, this little boy was born with a myriad of dietary restrictions.

Once his family connected with Mama's Kitchen, they began to receive daily meals. After receiving meals for quite a while, the family was invited to speak at one of Mama's fundraising and awareness events. The mom got up in front of the attendees and spoke about how desperate she had been for help and how much her family had struggled to pay the bills and keep up with a healthy family life. She spoke about how much of the burden was lifted when she contacted Mama's, a favor she was and forever will be thankful for.

Aimee's friend and coworker, Roger, delivered meals almost every day to various clients. Roger developed a very deep friendship with a woman named Ellie. Roger knew how Ellie was doing just from looking at her. Every time he visited her, he saw her state of isolation and never ceased trying to alleviate a bit of the loneliness she had to endure. Eventually, with medical help and support shown through friendship and food, Ellie began to feel more like herself again. Aimee commented, "This is very common, volunteers or employees becoming stable, kind, and loving figures for those we deliver to." The work Mama's Kitchen was doing really had the power to elicit confidence and rekindle hope.

Aimee explained that as a fundraiser, you have to wholeheartedly believe in the work done by the organization to truly sell your mission. "Eventually, you start to feel the mission in your veins. It becomes part of your DNA. When you're talking to someone about how they should invest, it's about the impact stories: the people changed through the difference you are making," she commented. Fully engulfed in the mission of Mama's, Aimee never questioned her impact.

However, Aimee did admit that although her work was meaningful, it became a lot to deal with on a few occasions. "I wanted to quit sometimes. Unfortunately, burnout plagues many in our field. Luckily, I had a really kind and caring boss who understood how to avoid this, because he had been doing it for a long time." Aimee's boss, Executive Director Alberto Cortés, used to say an organization often takes on the attributes of the problems they are trying to solve. Aimee agreed that this is unfortunately sometimes the case.

"At times in my career when I have tried to change course, I've always returned to this idea that this is who I am meant to be: a person who has a desire to have social impact in my work. If people like me, those with this desire, aren't the ones doing it, then it would not be a world I would really want to walk around in," Aimee confessed. In other words, if you have a desire to do something about the injustice swarming around you, then do it. Do not leave room for ill-intended people to pry off of the work you could be putting your heart and soul into.

After leaving Mama's Kitchen, Aimee moved on to become the codirector of development at another nonprofit in San Diego, Just in Time for Foster Youth. Just in Time focuses on curating a caring and welcoming community for former foster youth.[66]

---

66   Just in Time for Foster Youth. "Just in Time for Foster Youth | JIT." [online] Available at: https://www.jitfosteryouth.org/ [Accessed 4 Dec. 2019].

She stayed at Just in Time for a year and a half before transitioning to her current occupation as a freelance consultant. Now, instead of working with only one organization, she provides grant writing, event planning, and development strategies for various nonprofits in San Diego County.

For her more developed clients, Aimee's focus typically lies in grant writing and event planning. For smaller, developing clients, she helps mostly with development strategy, as many do not have their own development department. Most small nonprofits begin because the people who founded them are dedicated and passionate about their mission, but they often need organizational guidance, and that is where people like Aimee step in.

"It is a really different experience" being a contractor rather than an employee in a nonprofit organization, Aimee divulged. Grant writing is a highly desirable skill to have in a lot of different arenas. In fact, according to Aimee, this skill is definitely in demand. There are many different types of grant writing, depending on the audience and type of funder (government, corporate, foundation, etc.). As a grant writer who works in a specific nonprofit, as Aimee used to do for Mama's Kitchen and Just in Time, you are crafting and selling one mission through different avenues of impassioned persuasion. As a contract grant writer, Aimee provides her knowledge and expertise from a more distant perspective, recommending steps to amplify each client's mission.

At this stage in her career and life, Aimee loves this position because she can choose who she works with. She stated, "I have done this long enough, and I had always wanted to get to a place in my career where I could work anywhere. I know what I am doing, I can go in and really help organizations in a different, more beneficial way."

Reflecting on her experiences in the nonprofit world, Aimee confessed how her personal identity had, at one time, been too wrapped up in her work. "When I felt like the work I was doing didn't matter or I saw things I felt were really wrong, it really ended my hope in a lot of ways. I had an existential crisis about it all and went through a huge grieving period. I was so attached that I blended my work and my identity. I had a hard time putting work away. It simply wasn't healthy." Around this time, Aimee received one of the best pieces of advice that eventually caused her to see how damaging it was to get overly attached to your work.

One day, in response to her consuming state of stress, a coworker at Mama's Kitchen commented that she was working at Mama's Kitchen, not Aimee's Kitchen. "Honestly, that was liberating for me. It felt less like a diss and more like permission not to feel responsible for keeping all four walls up." Aimee grasped the idea that if she failed, it would be okay. She could think of new, creative ways to do her job and would soon find a new solution to the problem if she gave it time.

Aimee's ability to detach her identity from her work empowered her to do the work in a different, more effective way. By not assuming one hundred percent of the blame and responsibility if things don't go right, especially when participating in a field as emotionally trying as hers, burnout is less probable. Instead of feeling weighed down by the responsibility you have convinced yourself you must carry, you can focus on the elements of your identity that propel your work. Hone in on what makes you *you*: your kindness, empathy, and whatever else causes you to choose a life dedicated to enriching the lives of others.

If you are a person like Aimee who is always there for others, please know that you must not allow your care for others to overshadow your care for yourself. No, instead, you were made to care so that your life can flourish with substance. The way you interact with others makes them feel seen and paramount, even if only for a moment. You give so much to those around you, but you must give your heart a rest so that it can create more. Carve out the time you need to foster enough love and care to touch all those who need it without emptying before you, yourself, are lathered in it. Know that your kind words matter and the way you treat people will forever be imprinted in the fabric of their confidence, even if they don't acknowledge or express it.

But the way you treat yourself is where the true beauty lies. The way you love yourself will be the stimulus those around you need to transform the quality and longevity of their own happiness. And that, as a person who cares so deeply, is your greatest power. Use it.

THE LAND OF BROKEN DREAMS

———

Doniece Sandoval was living in San Francisco in 2011 when the economy plummeted. Throughout that year, she watched as three of her older African American neighbors were evicted from their homes because of the rising rental rates in the area.

All three of these close neighbors were forced to look for alternative housing. Although these men first sought refuge in homeless shelters, they were immediately placed on a long waiting list. Many people in this situation had no other choice but to take to the streets. Seeing the lives of the people she lived next to for years uprooted in a matter of days, Doniece immediately became deeply attuned to the overwhelming homelessness around her.

Doniece shared a memory with me that she defined as a pivotal moment in deciding to work to alleviate some of the burdens of the houseless population. A cab ride in 2013 took her into a downtown neighborhood in San Francisco called the Tenderloin. As they drove through the city, the cab driver said something to Doniece that she will never forget.

He turned his head toward her and wryly said, "Welcome to the land of broken dreams."

This comment stuck with her, as his words were jarring in their straightforwardness and disheartening validity. Sitting in the cab that day, she made up her mind. She decided she would do something more. "From that moment forward," she said, "I began to keep my eyes open. I'm an ideas person, and I knew that, eventually, I'd see a need that wasn't being met or a way to meet one better."

Months later, while walking in the design district of the city, Doniece passed a woman who was muttering over and over that she would never be clean. While she knew her words likely had many meanings, they made Doniece question what that woman's chances were of getting physically clean, because every visibly unhoused person she saw struggled with hygiene to some extent. Later that night, fueled by sadness and a desire to make a difference, she researched homelessness in San Francisco.

Doniece discovered that one of the harshest issues that homeless people deal with on a daily basis is, indeed, their inability to keep up with their personal hygiene. In fact, she found out that over seven thousand unhoused people in the San Francisco area alone were struggling with hygiene. At the time, only sixteen showers were available in the city for the unsheltered community. From these disheartening realizations, Doniece thought of an idea that would soon become the premise of Lava Mae.

In essence, Lava Mae is an organization with teams in San Francisco, Los Angeles, and Oakland that refurbishes old buses and transforms them into transportable showers. They open up these showers to anyone and everyone, allowing those on the streets to feel clean in a way many have not been used to for a while.[67]

Although the idea and planning stage of Lava Mae began in 2013, the program actually launched in June 2014. When Lava Mae first began, they used buses that were each equipped with two full showers. However, as they grew, they began converting to commercial shower trailer models. These commercial rigs have three full bathrooms, a positive upgrade they had not initially anticipated.

Within a month or so of the launch date of Lava Mae, Doniece and some of her team members met Marty. Marty was a young man who came to San Francisco from Detroit after he had been promised a job as a machinist. However, it took him a while to get to the city because he did not have much money at all. By the time he finally gathered up enough money to travel to San Francisco, his promised job was taken away. Unfortunately, another prospective candidate had replaced him.

Marty used nearly all of the money he had to get to the city that promised him a new life, so he ended up on the streets. He was undeterred at first, sure that he would be able to find another job as a machinist since the industry was booming at the time. Each day that he stayed on the streets, however, he became dirtier and less presentable.

Marty soon found himself in a rut, unable to change the perception of ruggedness that made him far less appealing to employers. One day, Marty found a flyer giving out the details about Lava Mae. Once he found their location, he showered with Lava Mae for about two weeks. A few weeks

---

67 Lava Mae. "Lava Mae." [online] Available at: https://lavamae.org/san-francisco/ [Accessed 4 Dec. 2019].

after his showers, Marty returned to the organization and told Doniece that he had found a job and was saving up money to soon be placed in a home. Later, Marty eventually started to work for Tesla, a well-known American automotive and energy company. Marty's story is a powerful example of how a simple shower can help to remove obstacles and enable someone to truly turn their life around.

In 2018, a man named Luis came up to Doniece on one of Lava Mae's shower days and introduced himself. He told her that six months ago when he was on the streets, he was so full of despair that he was truly ready to end his own life. He felt trapped in the cycle of homelessness and saw no clear way of escaping. Around that time, he was walking around Tenderloin and saw Lava Mae.

Before Luis approached the vans, he stood and watched as people entered the buses. As they exited the buses with wet hair, large smiles, and newfound postures, they all had a look of radiating joy and relief on their faces that wasn't there before they had entered. It dawned on him that he himself had not worn this look for quite some time. With nothing to lose, Luis got into the line for a shower.

"He told me about the indescribable feeling he felt in the moment that the water first hit his face," reminisced Doniece. As the dirt left his skin, he was stripped of all the despair and sadness that had coated his body for far too long. From that day on, Luis showered with Lava Mae every day, chasing that feeling that provided an escape from the overwhelming sense of darkness that had been lingering over him. Luis eagerly told Doniece that at the end of the next month, he was getting placed in a home.

Doniece also spoke fondly about a woman named Mary who came to take showers with Lava Mae. Mary had a disability and was in a wheelchair. For a while, Mary had been living in a women's center that ended up being far too dangerous to live in. This lady faced not only the challenge of being disabled but also of being a woman in an unsafe and hostile environment.

When Mary first came to shower with Lava Mae, she took about thirty minutes, a little longer than their guests usually spent inside the bus. To accommodate individuals like Mary, all of Lava Mae's buses and commercial shower trailers have a disability stall. Little did they know at the time, this thirty-minute shower was an incredibly emotional experience for Mary.

She exited the bus in a fit of tears. She told Doniece and the rest of the staff why she was crying. She looked at them and expressed how this was the first humane experience she had been a part of since the moment she became unhoused. Throughout the entire year that Mary showered with Lava Mae, Doniece and the staff watched as she transformed from a broken-down person to someone who radiated positivity. Mary connected with many of Lava Mae's other guests and transferred her hope onto others. She soon served as a visual reminder of the positive change that can take place when shelterless people are treated like actual human beings.

These are just a few of the stories that prove how transformative Lava Mae's work truly is. I asked Doniece if there were homeless people that, after having showered with Lava Mae, decided to volunteer with them. She happily stated that yes, they currently have sixteen "super guest" volunteers who bring a whole new personal element to the table.

Lava Mae launched another program in 2016 called Pop-Up Care Villages. With this program, twenty to twenty-five other organizations joined Lava Mae to provide a wide range of services for shelterless people that fall under three pillars: restorative, advancement, and community. Lava Mae contributes to the restorative section, providing showers, clothes, and more. The advancement pillar provides medical, dental, and legal aid to those in need. The third pillar, community, serves to support the teams working in the other sectors.

Doniece believes that the most beneficial way to combat issues is to initiate and situate an organization or group in the actual area that the problem exists. Therefore, in terms of Lava Mae, Doniece stated, "I do not anticipate any further expansions to other cities [aside from Los Angeles and Oakland]. Instead, the work that Lava Mae does has already inspired hygiene initiatives around the globe to start up in their home communities."

Lava Mae plans to stay focused in their three locations because those who work for them are all enduring a very high-touch, emotional job. Although it is emotionally rewarding, it can also be incredibly painful. They are working with vulnerable populations who are facing a vast number of difficult obstacles. Instead of growing the organization and spreading themselves too thin, Lava Mae hopes to improve their model and inspire the development of more organizations to take up similar lines of work.

In fact, on November 12, 2019, Lava Mae adopted its Radical Hospitality® approach to serving the shelterless community, transforming into a nonprofit accelerator by the name of Lava Mae^x. Lava Mae^x plans to expand its mission by training and creating strong connections with other compassionate and innovative organizations all around the world. Over the next five years, they aim to "fully train seventy-five communities around the globe to collectively serve one hundred thousand individual guests with programs rooted in Radical

Hospitality—a philosophy of meeting people wherever they are with extraordinary care."[68]

Doniece reflected on why she continues to work with this cause and what motivates her to not give up when the emotions become too much to handle. She explained with such clarity and assurance that "the access to water and sanitation is a basic human right. Until governments step up and address this lack of access to such fundamental rights, myself and the rest of those at Lava Mae feel compelled to fill that void."

* * *

My parents were the first people who taught me and my siblings about the need to care for even those we do not know. Growing up near Minneapolis, anytime we would go to the city, we would see people begging for money or other forms of assistance. While many people would pass a homeless individual on the street without looking twice, I have countless recollections of my dad doing just the opposite. He always said he felt the most compelled to help out when he saw someone who was physically sick or disabled. Though my dad would not give money to every single person who asked for it, he helped instill in me the desire to use my inherited privilege to give more than I take.

At one point during my childhood, my mom started to collect little bags my dad would get from his business flights. She created manna bags containing small yet useful items like toothbrushes, toothpaste, warm socks, nonperishable snacks,

68 Lava Mae. (2019). "Lava Mae relaunches as Lava Mae[x], a nonprofit accelerator for communities responding to the homelessness crisis." [online] Available at: https://lavamae.org/wp-content/uploads/2019/11/LMx-Press-Release.pdf?fbclid=IwARoXosxVRjM1xO kHQGWfwbVQfeAKgWFzSMnv2t Y655TuIXbXcxOJkcHCaXk [Accessed 4 Dec. 2019].

deodorant, napkins, and more. Eventually, she recognized the huge need for female hygiene products such as tampons and pads and started to include these additional items in many of her bags. For a long time, my mom kept at least one manna bag in her purse and a couple in the glove box of her car to always have accessible as she walked or drove through a homeless-dense area. The majority of the objects she would hand out were things that may not necessarily be the first item a person who can barely afford enough food for the day would buy, but items like these, especially ones that promote personal hygiene, are pertinent to one's self-esteem and make people feel more like the humans they are.

When my little brother, Cooper, moved with my parents from Barcelona to a town called Reardan, Washington, he became more aware of the huge shelterless community in the nearby city of Spokane. As a junior in high school and the new kid at school, he quickly recognized the huge potential of his fellow students and teachers. On the basis of his own will and eagerness to *do* something, he researched shelters in Spokane and immediately gravitated toward one called Crosswalk Youth Shelter. This particular shelter supports the houseless youth with the principal objective of "ending their homelessness and connecting them to stabilizing and supportive services."[69]

Cooper began an initiative to collect clothes. He emphasized the need for warm coats and socks, as Spokane gets extremely cold in the winter. Upon catching wind of this initiative, a staff member at his high school reached out and told him that a pile of winter jackets had been lying in their

69   Volunteers of America: Eastern Washington and Northern Idaho. "Volunteers of America." [online] *Crosswalk.* Available at: https://www. voaspokane.org/crosswalk [Accessed 4 Dec. 2019].

lost and found for months. After making announcements once again to make sure no one claimed these jackets, Cooper took them as well as a couple of boxes of donated clothes to Crosswalk.

I was with Cooper the day he dropped off these boxes at the shelter. To my surprise, Crosswalk had a very warm and inviting atmosphere. One of the little boys who greeted us at the door begged the supervisor to be the first to look through the boxes, attempting to convince him that his need for new warm socks was imperative.

Donating to those we see begging on the streets is a simple act that so many of us are capable of doing. A lot of people have the opinion that if they give money to someone on the streets, those people might simply use it to fuel an addiction. If this is something that deters you from helping at all, consider manna bags, donating clothes, or contributing to the expansion and growth of an organization like Lava Mae. There are other ways to help. You just have to be willing to see past stereotypes and realize that most homeless people merely yearn to remove themselves from their situation and be treated in a humane manner.

After talking to Doniece, I saw a common theme throughout everything she relayed to me about the efforts of her organization. As she noted, "Lava Mae is rooted in the idea that no small act of kindness goes unnoticed." Everyone dreams of doing something big to make a difference. However, Doniece recognizes that changing one person's world is often more attainable and just as noteworthy. She lives by the ripples of her small yet significant actions. Just by acknowledging a person's existence when they feel forgotten and shunned, you are giving that person a new light that has the potential to brighten up their entire world.

FOSTERING LITERACY IN THE DIGITAL AGE

———

Colin McElwee and David Risher had wonderful educational experiences and professional careers before realizing that they were missing something. Colin explained how, at one point in his life, he reflected on the good fortune he had and felt as though everything his fortuitous circumstances brought him was going to waste.

Colin began to fully utilize his resources and contacts by reforming his life mission. He soon concluded that he would use his luck by creating an organization that would benefit those who are born into less fortunate economic or social situations. Colin and his friend David got together and built their organization around a collaborative effort to benefit those in dire need of education.

"When I first started up Worldreader with David," Colin remarked, "I felt truly useful for the first time in my life."

Worldreader aims to improve literacy by providing members of underdeveloped nations access to e-readers, apps, and digital books. In nearly ten years, Worldreader has established

638 schools and libraries across the globe in an impressive forty-eight different countries.[70]

In the summer of 2017, I had the privilege of volunteering at Worldreader's office in Barcelona. While there, I had the pleasure of meeting the cofounder of the nonprofit, Colin McElwee. While my time there only lasted two-and-a-half months, my experience was eye-opening. I spent most of my volunteer time researching organizations in Jordan and India so Worldreader might forge more meaningful partnerships. Partner organizations are crucial to broaden any organization's outreach. One of Colin's key roles is deciding which organizations to reach out to.

Colin's idea of success erupted as a result of Worldreader's creation and growth and the feeling he gets when he knows his experience and work is meaningful. As Colin puts it, "A type of utilitarian value comes to life when working for an organization that helps desperate people in a very real and effective way."

Worldreader has four principal programs. The first consists of school reading programs that are centered around helping students excel in the classroom. The second program, library reading, shares vital tools and expertise with local librarians so they can expand the reading community. The third program is the lifelong reading program. This initiative utilizes "the Worldreader app, data analytics, and partnerships with publishers and mobile providers to empower youths and adults to access books on their mobile devices." This program was first established to extend people's involvement with reading long after they end their schooling.

---

70 Worldreader. "Creating A World Where Everyone Can Be A Reader." [online] *Worldreader*. Available at: https://www.worldreader.org/ [Accessed 4 Dec. 2019].

The fourth project is the pre-reading program or the parental engagement initiative. This initiative is operating in Delhi, India, and Amman, Jordan, where training manuals are created for members in these areas to use in teaching parents about reading with their kids outside of school. Colin touched on this program's significance. He explained, "We began this initiative by first considering the most effective way of shifting the responsibility of a child's literacy not only to the children themselves but also to their parents." Through programs like this, children's education and overall literacy skills are enhanced beyond what they learn in the classroom.

The program in Jordan, now called Worldreader Kids - Tuta Tuta, has been especially transformative because they work with the children of Syrian refugees. "People do not get out of refugee status quickly. In fact, the average time for someone to be a refugee is seventeen years. During these years, they often feel as though they have lost their past. Most of them have lost their homes, their friends, their loved ones . . . everything. The worst thing for a refugee to feel is that they have not only lost their past but that they have lost their future," Colin expressed. With their programs in Jordan, Worldreader hopes to use education to prevent this devastating prospect from developing into a reality.

One of the most crucial aspects of Worldreader's work is selecting the books they distribute. By collaborating with partner organizations in the targeted distribution area, Worldreader communicates with the local government. Essentially, the government has books they wish to be included in the libraries and schools of their country and will have the final say in the acceptance or denial of each book.

However, Worldreader has created a very thorough process of book selection. Volunteers or staff members read through each of the books and often select those most beneficial to the children who will read them. Colin added, "We are very thoughtful when choosing the books. We tend to choose short books, as nowadays people tend to be more data-driven. We also always seek out inviting covers and motivational titles."

When I was at Worldreader, we worked on selecting books to be given to Syrian refugee children in Jordan. We heavily emphasized choosing books that would help those who read them overcome trauma and PTSD issues, as many of the Syrian children endured horrible experiences during and after their escape from war-torn countries. The idea was—and still is—to create a collection of books that allow the children to feel seen, less alone, and hopeful about their future despite the situations they face.

Colin is passionate about selecting relevant and sensitive books. In fact, the importance of this selection process is illustrated by one particular story that has stuck with him to this day. While Colin was in Nairobi's largest slum, Kibera, in 2014, he visited a library Worldreader had built. On a Saturday during his visit, Colin remembers the library filled with nearly two hundred Kenyan girls wearing their school uniforms, which was the only nice outfit the majority of them owned. What amazed Colin to see was that all of these girls came to the library on one of their days off simply because they were genuinely eager to learn more.

That day, various people came in to talk to the uniformed girls about the power of education and inspirational stories of growth. "Throughout the day, I made a point of having conversations with the girls, asking them about themselves and their hopes and dreams. Upon finishing a conversation with a group of the girls, the head librarian came to talk with me. She found it wonderful that I was taking the time to talk with some of the girls and informed me that many of these young women had extremely tragic stories," said Colin.

The one story that struck Colin the hardest was about a fourteen-year-old girl who was born to a prostitute. This girl's mother left her on the streets. The girl lived her whole life being fostered by an assortment of families until one day her birth mother found her again.

When they were reacquainted, her mother was still a prostitute. She intended to persuade her daughter to become a prostitute. Although many other girls in similar positions may have not known how to avoid following in their mother's' footsteps, this young girl refused to subject herself to a life of prostitution and managed to escape.

When the girl told her story to the librarian, she stated how she had read a book about girls in positions like hers, those who have been pressured by their mothers or fathers to live a life they didn't dream of for themselves. The little girl in the book found a way out and refused her parents. This book, provided by Worldreader in one of the libraries they built, empowered this teenage girl. It taught her to not be afraid to chase a life she desired and fully deserved, a life that reaped the benefits of education.

Organizations like Worldreader inspire hope and the desire to better one's future through books. After hearing this story of empowerment through education, Colin knew their work truly does make a difference. If you can make that difference—if you can save one little girl from a vicious cycle of prostitution and objectification—why wouldn't you?

By providing an inkling of hope, you can find purpose in what you are doing. A definitive purpose lies within them and within you, and when coupled together, it can produce something life-changing.

MY AHA MOMENT

───

When Layla[71] was in her early twenties, she, her father, mother, and brother relocated from their birth country of Iraq to Greece where they stayed in refuge for about two-and-a-half years. In the late 1990s, Layla and her family were granted entry to the United States. They packed up their few belongings and resettled in California. A couple of years after arriving in California, Layla moved to Michigan where she gave birth to her two children.

In Michigan, Layla created a clothing business, tapping into one of the passions she held from a very young age. When she was a little girl in Iraq, she would play with dolls and use toilet paper to create beautiful wedding gowns. Stoking her young self's dreams, Layla decided to first focus on creating bridal dresses. When she moved back to San Diego, she brought her business with her. Although this business has now expanded its array of clothing styles, it still stands in Mission Valley, San Diego.

A couple of years after she moved back to San Diego, Layla met a nun at her local Christian church that told her

───

71 Names in this story were changed for security reasons.

about a local resettlement agency in the area. This agency is committed to aiding individuals who have been affected by conflict and disaster. They focus on contributing to their clients' survival, recovery, and quality of life improvement. At the time, this agency was desperately looking for a person who spoke Chaldean. Chaldean is a language spoken by a Catholic ethno-religious community that originates from northern Iraq.

Layla, a native Chaldean and Arabic speaker, was not interested in the position when the nun at her church first told her about it. She was quite content with her life as a designer and did not want to leave her business. However, after repetitive encouragement from the nun, Layla reluctantly agreed to give this agency a go. When she was there, she translated for two Chaldean refugees. These women spoke no other language and felt so thankful to finally be able to communicate their needs and the difficulties they were facing. Layla felt a sudden connection to these two ladies and helped them find an affordable apartment complex in El Cajon, a city on the eastern side of San Diego County.

The staff at this agency was floored to see the impact Layla was making on the lives of the clients and how much she helped them despite the fact that she was not even working for them. They begged her to join the team, explaining that with this position, she would be able to work directly with refugees and help them integrate into the community. Layla eventually agreed to sell her business and joined their resettlement team.

Layla has been a case manager at this agency for over thirteen years. She has helped countless refugees and individuals with Special Immigrant Visas (SIVs) resettle in San Diego. One of her many job duties is to pick up the families from the airport upon their arrival, welcoming them to their new and strange home. Layla also finds local affordable places to rent for her clients and prepares the home with furniture, supplies, and food. She aids them in dealing with lease agreements and helps them learn how to pay their rent, put down security deposits, and deal with application fees.

In addition, Layla supports her clients in applying for Medi-Cal, food stamps, cash aid, Social Security cards, school registration for children, entrance medical appointments, and much more. She also gives each client cultural orientation lessons and assessments to equip them with the knowledge necessary to live a safe and healthy life in the US. For clients with children under the age of five, Layla and the others at the resettlement department assist them in applying for infant and childcare through WIC.[72] In addition, those who are over the age of sixty-five are assisted with applying for Social Security insurance.

These duties all merely scratch the surface of the work Layla does every day. The number of clients she works with every month shifts depending on the political climate and how many cases are being accepted and distributed nationwide.

Layla explained that "many people come to the US thinking all of their problems are going to be solved." Many individuals don't realize that the hardships only continue . . . but that is where the staff tries to help. Layla elaborated, "We know how difficult it is because most of us have been through a similar situation, so we try to help in any way we can. Because as hard as it can be, we care, and that's why we do what we do."

In 2014, Layla was working with an Iraqi couple who was only one month away from receiving their green cards.

---

72   San Diego WIC. "Women, Infants & Children." [online] *Sandiegowic. org*. Available at: http://sandiegowic.org/ [Accessed 7 Dec. 2019].

One day, the husband came to her office and told her, "Layla, I am not really happy in the United States. I am going to go back to Iraq."

Layla knew that part of the reason why he was unhappy was that he had yet to find a job. At the time, the man was over fifty years old. For many refugees and asylum seekers the agency works with, when they are over fifty, it is a lot more difficult for them to find jobs, especially if they do not speak the language very well. Facing both of these barriers to integration, the client felt that his best option was to leave everything he had worked for and go with his wife back to their country.

The man explained to Layla that he felt like he was failing. Concerned, Layla asked him why he would want to go back to Iraq after everything he had been through. The man explained that back in Iraq, he owned land and had a good job that allowed him to provide for himself and his family. Now, in the United States, he felt guilty because he had to rely on his two sons who had migrated a couple of years before. He felt especially wary of leaning on his sons since they both only worked minimum-wage jobs at a coffee shop and at Burger King.

The man earnestly begged Layla to help him and his family get plane tickets to leave. Layla, knowing quite well that this would be possible, told him honestly, "If you leave, you will be making the biggest mistake of your life." The man denied the validity of this comment, declaring it was what he had to do.

Layla asked the man if she could talk to his wife to see what she had to say. Later that day, the couple returned. Layla looked at the wife for answers. The wife admitted that she did not want to leave but said she had to do what her husband wished. With this, Layla upped her convincing. Eventually, she got them to wait at least until they received their green cards.

A week or two before the couple secured their green cards, ISIS took over a little village in Iraq: the very one the couple was trying to go back to a few weeks prior. ISIS swept the village, took everything from the civilians' homes, and bombed left and right. This attack resulted in the death of twelve policemen and several civilians.[73]

A few months after the couple accepted their green cards, Layla was at a friend's wedding when she saw this family for the first time since the conversation in which she had successfully convinced them to stay in the US. She watched as the once angry and sorrowful husband danced happily with his family. In the midst of a fruitful dance, the man caught Layla's eye. He rushed over to her and said, "Layla, is that you?"

"Yes," she replied.

"Layla, I am going to make statues in your name! You are the reason I am still alive with my family. If I hadn't listened to you at that time, I would have now been dead."

Although this may seem like a simple act of kindness, a common deed among caseworkers, it was charged with something far grander. As the man acknowledged on that wedding day, her argument to make him stay is what kept him alive.

One time, Layla worked with an Afghan family that entered the States with a US tie. A US tie is a family member who is already situated in the US and often helps the family

---

73 Hassan, G. (2014). *Iraq dislodges insurgents from city of Samarra with airstrikes.* [online] Rueters. Available at: https://www.reuters.com/article/us-iraq-security/iraq-dislodges-insurgents-from-city-of-samarra-with-airstrikes-idUSKBN0EG1RG20140605 [Accessed 7 Dec. 2019].

integrate into the community. In this case, the family's tie was living in San Diego but did not have enough space or money to host them for longer than a couple of days.

When Layla visited the family for a twenty-four-hour home visit, they cried and told her they had made a mistake by leaving their country. They had not realized how expensive it would be in San Diego and how little they would be able to rely on their US tie or their very limited English capabilities. They were concerned about how to pay for everything, especially housing. Layla assured them that she would find an affordable apartment for them in an Afghan ethnic enclave so that they could find comfort in their new community.

The family, like many other refugee families, had come with no money. Many refugees decide to leave everything behind because this is the only way they can receive full food, medical, and cash assistance. With no money and no jobs, they didn't know what they could do. Layla found them an apartment that eventually agreed to take them with a loan. Within ten days, Layla spoke with the other departments in the agency and managed to secure cash assistance that covered their rent for the first couple of months, alleviating some of the pressure they felt and ultimately allowed them the time to find fitting jobs.

For the past three years, Layla has worked alongside another caseworker named Hamid. Hamid was born in Afghanistan and remembered constantly migrating between his birth country and Pakistan. Reflecting on his childhood, Hamid remarked, "I never really went to school when I was in Afghanistan." At one time, Hamid remembered having a classroom with no roof. With this inconvenient structure, classes would be canceled anytime it rained or was too hot.

As conflict arose in Afghanistan, his family knew they needed to move. When he was only sixteen years old, Hamid, his eighteen-year-old sister, and his mother gained refugee status in the US and were sent to Salt Lake City, Utah. When Hamid arrived in Salt Lake City, he spoke very little English and struggled to integrate into the community. Once he settled into his new home, Hamid took a placement exam at the local school. Although he was sixteen, he was placed in fourth grade, causing him to feel even more out of place and ostracized by his peers.

Despite the difficulties thrown his way, Hamid worked diligently to move from grade to grades and eventually went to community college before finishing his education at a four-year university.

Before holding a permanent position at the refugee resettlement agency, Hamid interned with a different department. However, in 2016, he was hired to work with Layla and the others in the resettlement department. Reflecting on his work, Hamid explained, "A lot of clients don't actually tell us about their life stories. I think sometimes they come to us with the mind-set that if they don't give us all the information, then they will get more of our services." However, when they do open up, Hamid feels like he is able to help them more wholeheartedly.

During the first year Hamid worked as a resettlement caseworker, he received an SIV family from Afghanistan that consisted of a husband, wife, and their seven children. The husband was the only one in the family that spoke English. When Hamid was looking for apartments for the family, he struggled to find one in their budget. A law in California prohibits a family of nine from living in an apartment with two or fewer rooms. Therefore, he had to find one with three bedrooms, which was very difficult, given their budget.

The cheapest option Hamid eventually found was an apartment in El Cajon that was still around $300 more than they were getting through public benefits. However, with no other options, the family ultimately agreed to sign the lease. The father immediately went to Hamid's agency for employment assistance. He went to the Public Consulting Group (PCG) and enrolled in English-language classes, yet he was still unable to get a job. Four or five months went by, and the father came to Hamid's office to tell him he really didn't know if he could continue. He was the only one in his family that was fit to work. In fact, all seven of his children were below the legal working age of eighteen.

Back in Afghanistan, the man was a truck driver and a welder. Hamid realized the untapped potential within him and told him that he must stop looking for jobs that didn't fit him (line cook, cashier, etc.) and look into becoming a truck driver again. The man followed this advice and went back to PCG where they helped him enroll in truck school. He already clearly knew how to drive a truck, but he needed to learn the rules specific to California. After a few months of training, he obtained a new valid license. The day he received his license, a trucking company reached out and hired him on the spot.

From this job, the man was able to make nearly $8,000 every month. With this amount of money, he was now able to make all of his monthly rent payments, support his family, and get off of public assistance altogether.

This man profusely thanked Hamid, as he was the one who basically coached him through every situation of doubt and frustration. Hamid commented on their relationship now. "I see him around a lot, actually, as we are both part of the Afghan community here. Whenever he sees me helping out a new client, he always says, 'Oh, you're lucky that he is your caseworker.' These connections with past clients remind me that what we are doing truly makes a difference."

I have gotten the privilege to work alongside both Layla and Hamid, and I can assure you that these were just a couple of the hundreds of lives they have both touched on a very profound level. They care so deeply for their clients that they'll end up spending hours or days going the extra mile just to make sure these individuals are getting the support they need during this transitional period of life.

* * *

I think that neither Layla nor Hamid give themselves enough credit for what they do. Working on their team for a couple of months, I witnessed the way their clients depended on them and how much they helped even when it far surpassed the duties outlined in their job description. Although Layla and Hamid's department is only meant to work with each case for the first three months, oftentimes past clients would come in asking for advice or help with something many months or even years after they arrived in the US. Time and time again, I have seen these two help as much as they can, giving their all to this work, as much as it sometimes drains them to do so.

As a refugee client services intern, I assisted Layla and Hamid in most of their duties. One of the most transformative elements of this internship was how often I got to meet and work directly with the clients. One of my main duties included driving and accompanying clients to their appointments for health checkups, welfare, WIC, and elsewhere. By meeting the clients themselves, I put faces and personalities to the names of the files I would assemble with I-94s, EADs,

AR-11s, assurance forms, biodata, arrival notifications, US tie agreements, and other important documents.

One of my favorite parts of this internship was assisting my supervisors with setting up the family apartments. We would go shopping for a set list of items, pick up donations, and then set up the apartment so it was move-in ready.

On my very first day of the internship, Layla took me to go grocery shopping for an incoming case of nine. As they were from the Democratic Republic of Congo, she assured me that they would love a freshly cooked white fish, as it would remind them of a common dish from their home country. We went to a local ethnic grocery market to pick up the fish and other staple food items. We then took the food to their two apartments and set up their dining tables with the fish settled neatly in the center. With this setup, we hoped to create a feeling of warmth and comfort that would greet them for their first night in America after a few long days of traveling.

This family later became the most frequent case I worked with. The family consisted of a father and his seven children, one of whom was already settled in San Diego, and one grand-child. The mother of this family and another daughter had been left behind in a refugee camp in Uganda. According to the second oldest son, Samuel, his younger sister had been labeled disabled and therefore "unfit" to be granted refuge in the United States: a shocking and disheartening decision that led to the separation of this loving and close-knit family.

All of the children who arrived in our office spoke con-versational English, which allowed me to connect with them on a deeper level than some of the other clients I worked with. One day, when I was driving them to their medical appoint-ments, Jude and Esther, two of the older siblings of the family, expressed how difficult it was to stay optimistic even though they had already made it to the US. Jude explained how bored he was, as he had no friends and no way to occupy his time.

"Riding here in this car has been the best thing of my week," I still remember him saying.

One day, Esther, the mother of the baby of the family, entered the office when both my supervisors were away. I was the only one there working on paperwork and walked her through a cultural orientation training. This training covered the basic rules and tips for living safely in the US. Afterward, I tested her on her knowledge through a short ten-question exam. After we finished this examination, we had a casual conversation. I always related to Esther and loved speaking with her about her passions and dreams. We seemed to relate in a lot of arbitrary yet beautiful ways and shared the meager age of twenty.

I remember asking her that day how her job search was going. She replied that it was unsuccessful so far, and she was unsure that any job would accept her.

I assured her that she would be able to find one with time and even suggested she try to get a job where her brother Marc was working. Marc had moved to San Diego a couple of months before the rest of the family and had already begun working at a local 7-Eleven gas station.

In response, Esther looked at me and told me that she was pregnant for a second time. Without her father's knowing, she had traveled to San Diego during her first trimester and was certain her belly would begin to show soon. She started to tear up as she explained that this would be her and her husband's second child. Her husband was still in a refugee camp in Uganda, patiently awaiting acceptance to join Esther and her family. She told me that she didn't know if her husband would arrive before the baby was born and was concerned that no one would hire her if they found out she was pregnant.

During this whole conversation, Esther was convinced that she didn't even want her caseworker, Layla, to know she was pregnant. She was afraid that Layla would be mad at her for keeping it quiet for so long and would tell her secret to her father. After much reassuring, I convinced her to tell Layla by explaining that together we would be able to help her get assistance once she opened up about her pregnancy. Later that same day, Esther agreed to tell Layla. Once she did, I quickly booked her an appointment with WIC to receive prenatal care assistance.

Although I wasn't able to personally take Esther to her first WIC appointment, I know she felt a sense of relief when she finally confided in somebody and received valuable support and care. Esther is a strong woman who had to grow up far faster than I did, leaving me to be continuously astonished by her never-faltering resilience.

Little moments and conversations I had with members of this family taught me how similar we all are. I think back to when Samuel showed off his red shoes, trying (yet failing) to convince me that they were in style. I think back to the orange juice Emmanuel, their father, offered me every time I would enter his apartment as he earnestly expressed that he liked to treat his guests even though he was unable to afford a drink of higher caliber. I think back to the various times Jude, Marc, Samuel, or Raoul rushed to get to the door before me just so they could hold it open as I walked through.

This family showed me what most people truly desire is to be happy and safe. Together they fled persecution and left their friends and part of their family to secure a potentially more prosperous future. And yet they still managed to smile, joke around, and show boundless benevolence toward me and others they encountered. Thinking about it now, this family was my aha moment—my wake-up call, my intimate source of understanding the situation—my hope.

PEACEFUL RUINS

———

I met Maisara Sassi in 2014, the year I moved to Barcelona, Spain. She was in my grade at ASB and was one of the first people to make me feel accepted. When I first met her, all I noticed was her smile, the way she joked around, and her emanating kindness toward me and everyone else around her. Our humor, interests, and the way we treated people seemed so similar that when we discovered we had the same birthday, we declared to one another we must be twins.

Thinking back years later to my initial opinion of Maisara, with our mirrored attributes and outlook on life, I would have never guessed how different our childhoods had been. I grew up in a middle-class Catholic family, moving from Spokane, Washington, to Hudson, Wisconsin, when I was five years old. In elementary and middle school, I played a good number of sports, knew virtually everyone in my small town, and had a close-knit immediate family. I played in the woods with my friends, went to the movies, and loved building snow forts in my cul-de-sac with neighbors. I never experienced anything particularly traumatizing, and for the most part, that era of my life was quite normal.

Maisara grew up with a similar close-knit family but in a very different place than my Wisconsin suburb. Maisara was born and raised in a Muslim household in the North African capital of Tripoli, Libya. Nevertheless, when reflecting on her early childhood, Maisara also remembers her upbringing to have been quite normal and peaceful. She grew up playing piano and tennis and riding horses around her grandparents' farm. Quality time with her large family was near and dear to her heart. She and her family would often go camping under the stars in the desert, throw festive BBQ parties, and host seasonal community celebrations. She went to a local school, hung out with her friends, and was slowly learning what it meant to be an older sister.

However, when Maisara was only eleven years old, her life took an unexpected turn. A war broke out in Libya as part of the Arab Spring on February 17, 2011. As Maisara noted, "Not only did Libya witness its first-ever civil war, but it also became a battleground for international powers to do as they wished to achieve their own interests."

For the first two months of the war, Maisara's parents tried their hardest to hide the severity of what was happening from their children. "But then, eventually, more of my daily routine started to change. At some point, I stopped going to school, and that's when I first figured out something was wrong," explained Maisara. As Tripoli progressively became more dangerous, Maisara's parents decided to move their family to their grandparents' estate located about an hour away from the city in a town called Surman.

At some point during the three months Maisara and her family stayed with her grandparents, her dad's job as an architect was halted because of the war. As a result, he had to leave the country in search of a safer and more stable place for their family. His time away was supposed to last four days, but it was cut short and he returned to Libya on the second day, June 20, 2011. Upon his return, he picked up the rest of his family from their grandparents' estate and they went back to their house in Tripoli.

That same night, sitting in the comfort of their own home, Maisara vividly remembers her mom receiving an absurd amount of phone calls. They eventually turned on the news and saw their grandparents' house, the place they had just left, appear on the television screen.

The family estate had been bombed eight times by the American and Canadian forces of NATO. Maisara and her family watched the news in horror as the reporters explained on national television that they were unsure if anybody at the estate made it out alive.

Each rocket that hit the house had weighed a thousand kilograms. Right after hearing the devastating news, Maisara's mother bolted to the car. What would normally have been an hour drive took three hours because so many guards blocked every street. Maisara added, "Thinking about it now makes me so sad. She didn't know if her parents were alive. For all she knew, they and all her nieces, nephews, and siblings were dead."

Maisara's paternal grandmother ended up coming to their house in Tripoli to stay the night with the children because they were all too young, vulnerable, and innocent to even begin to understand what had just happened to their own blood relatives. At the time, Maisara's brother was eight years old and her sister was three. Maisara still remembers how the adults in her family tried their best to protect her and her siblings by not telling them what was truly happening.

"What they failed to take into account was that the horrors of war seep into the consciousness of all its victims. War does not empathize with age," she confessed.

The next morning, Maisara and her siblings found out three of their baby cousins, their aunt-in-law who was pregnant with twins, their grandma's sister, and some of the farmers and security guards that worked on the farm were all killed by the bombs.

In remembering her family members who died, Maisara commented on the symbolic and almost otherworldly elucidations of their names. One of her cousins was called Salam. The literal translation of "Salam" from Arabic is "peace." To say this little girl lived up to her name would be an understatement.

"She added more value and significance to the name with her angelic and celestial persona. She was soft-spoken, graceful, and never demanded attention," said Maisara. Salam lived happily with five brothers as the only girl. According to Maisara, she was the epitome of an angel, her mother's right hand and always her grandfather's favorite.

A week before Salam was murdered, she told her mother, "I really want to see Prophet Mohammed, Mama." Less than a week after, she got to see him in heaven.

Maisara's second female cousin who died in the bombings was named Khalida. Khalida in Arabic means "the everlasting" or "the eternal life."

Maisara expressed, "She did indeed have a very everlasting impression on whoever she met. Khalida was a very lively, buoyant, and bright soul. She was curious and often left adults speechless with the intelligence embedded in her questions."

Khalida was the older sister of Khweldi, the youngest of the three cousins who fell victim to the bombs.

"Khweldi was a literal ray of sunshine. The constant smile that never left his face could light up the whole world."

Little Khweldi had just turned four on the night he was murdered in his sleep. What did he wish for on his birthday?

"I wish for the war to end," he said, a phrase that he had heard so much came to him so casually as he blew out the candles on his fourth and last birthday.

Salam, Khalida, and Khweldi's story touched and grieved many around the nation. Soon after their deaths were announced, they became the youngest "national heroes and martyrs" in Libya. They also became the eternal image of the stolen childhoods of the war.

After the air strike, Maisara's parents realized how dangerous their beloved homeland was becoming. Civilian communities were being bombed by NATO. The old regime responded because NATO was there to aid the rebels against the leader of the country, Muammar Gaddafi. As a result, tension increased on both sides.

A week after the bombing, the family fled the country with Maisara's aunt, mother of the deceased Salam. Years after the death of her daughter, Maisara's aunt gave birth to another girl, but she refused to give her the same name as Salam. Instead, she named her Hala, meaning "beauty" or "the beauty of life" with the hope that this child too would embody the meaning of her assigned name.

Maisara reflected on this experience of fleeing. "Leaving Libya meant leaving the rest of my family behind and not knowing if we would ever be reunited, leaving friends that I already lost all contact with due to the war, and leaving the rubble of the home I was raised in."

Maisara and her family ended up going to Tunisia, a country in northern Africa bordering Libya. The family stayed in the capital, Tunis, for a little over a month until fleeing to Morocco where they stayed and lived for over half a year. In August of the following year, the family flew to Spain where they hoped to build a more permanent life.

The whole experience of having family members die, becoming internally displaced, and then fleeing to three different countries in the time span of a year caused Maisara and her siblings to grow up faster than they would have otherwise. "I don't think any kid should have to see or endure any stage of war . . . because it really messes with you. And I luckily didn't have to experience it for nearly as long as many who couldn't leave. But I did have my family murdered, and honestly, it took years to finally see and understand how that transformed me in so many different ways." She confessed, "It felt so crazy to see the numbers of those killed in the tragedies in Libya but so much worse knowing my family made up some of those numbers."

When I met Maisara, she was in the long process of recovery she did not even realize she was in. She was smiling and befriending me, someone from the very country who sent the planes that killed her family. And she never thought of me differently. After the first time Maisara told me what had happened to her family, I remember being shocked. For some reason I cannot clearly articulate, a part of me almost felt guilty, not sure how she could find it within her to be friends with me, an American. She assured me that she and her family believe in the goodness of all people and recognize that what happened is not my fault nor the fault of my people. Rather, it was a byproduct of an ugly war, and they do not hold hostility toward Americans for the unprecedented tragedy inflicted upon their people.

When I first went over to Maisara's apartment in Barcelona when we were in the ninth grade, her family welcomed me with open arms. Her mom greeted us at the door, filling our stomachs with amazing Libyan dishes. One time after I spent the day at their apartment, her dad offered to drive me home. In the car, he expressed how happy he was that his daughter and I were friends. He explained to me that, whether we thought of it this way or not, we were exploring what it meant to have a meaningful and mutually beneficial intercultural friendship. He supposed it would be a friendship that taught us both something invaluable. He could not have been more spot on.

Maisara's dad founded a construction company in Libya right after he graduated from university with a degree in architecture. Since the war, his business has been working to rebuild Libyan infrastructure. Maisara's dad, now working from Barcelona, focuses on applying for and receiving grants from the United Nations to use toward his rebuilding strategies. Simultaneously, his brother, who still lives in Libya, works on managing the actual construction of apartments, schools, libraries, and hospitals.

Maisara explained that for her dad, this job has definitely been rewarding but also extremely trying. Rebels in the area of their rebuilding have started to harass some of the business's workers at gunpoint, threatening to tear down all they have built if they do not hire them on the project. Many of these threats are made in attempts to gain money because the individuals who make them often come from nothing. With the instability in the country, many people unfortunately get away with acts like this because no real governing body will punish them.

On Maisara's paternal side, all of her family members still live in Libya. "You might think something like electricity cuts is not a huge deal. But my family and the others still in Libya have to deal with it nearly every day." Her family has to deal with these electricity cuts in the burning heat of the summer and during Ramadan, a sacred time for those of the Islamic faith. During Ramadan, fasting is practiced from dawn till dusk, making the cuts even more difficult and physically draining.

Maisara's beloved country of origin might never heal completely. Little by little, the elements of the post-war era have become less and less of a shock. "Now when I call my grandma, I am genuinely expecting her to say, 'Oh the power was out from this time to this time.' So in an odd and saddening way, it is actually becoming normal for me, just from hearing about the reality of their every day."

Not only are Maisara's relatives in Libya having to deal with problems like electricity cuts, but they also face serious threats to their everyday safety. In fact, on December 2, 2015, three of Maisara's second cousins' safety was not just threatened, it was stripped away.

It began as a day just like the rest. The three children were riding in the back of their car with their mother and driver on their way to school. As the family arrived at the gate of the school, a van carrying armed men pulled up next to them. Some of the men fired at the family's car while two others snuck up to it and grabbed the children from the back seat. The children were smuggled into the van, and the armed men sped off before either the mother or the driver could do anything but scream and cry.

The driver had been shot five times during the abduction. As days moved on, the state of his wounds only deteriorated. The driver's festering gun wounds brought to light how terribly inadequate Libyan health institutions' medical resources were compared to those in more stable nations.

On the day the children were kidnapped, the armed men called their father to let him know his children were "safe" but "sick." The father was devastated and had never received any personal threats in the past, leaving him to wonder why his family was chosen for this catastrophe. At this point, no ransom money was demanded. Instead, the children's father and mother had no choice but to wait and wallow in their misery and accumulating fear.

Eventually, the kidnappers requested LYD 20 million (Libyan dinars) as a ransom for the return of the children, the equivalent of about $14 million.

The children's parents tried everything they could to track their abducted children. However, the parents saw the authorities take no pressing actions.

Due to the lack of governmental aid, the parents resorted to the media and large news channels to help spread the word about their missing children. The media helped, but not to the extent they were hoping for. "Even though the case received the public's sympathy," Maisara said, "the parents and the public could only do so much. Hence why this story, like many others, has a sickening and heartbreaking ending."

During this time, a well-known gang had been at the center of countless armed clashes with Western militia forces in Surman. This gang was suspected of being responsible for the murder of over thirty people and the kidnapping of fifteen.

In the year following the abduction of Maisara's second cousins, another terrible clash occurred between the gang and the Western militia. Seven kidnappers in the gang were ultimately captured. Through interrogation, some members of the gang eventually confessed information regarding the whereabouts of the three children. Despite this lead, authorities failed once again to make any real progress on the investigation. Many believed that one of the main reasons why they hesitated to put pressure on the case was because they feared that the leader of the powerful gang would come after them.

After years of never giving up hope in the consistent attempt to find their children, in 2018, the parents were notified that the bodies of their three little ones had been found. After a forensic investigation, it was confirmed that the children had been dead since 2015, the year they had initially been kidnapped.

As soon as the news of the deaths reached the Supreme Council of State in Libya, they immediately sent out statements of condolences to the family and mandated that security authorities must take more extreme measures in future cases. Unfortunately, frequent child abductions continue to be part of the reality of life in Libya.

The current situation is still not entirely safe. Even though they have an internationally recognized government, a huge political divide still drives a lot of the tension, especially in Tripoli.

Regardless of the current state of her country, Maisara has relentlessly been begging her parents to go back to Libya for years now. In fact, she has not been back to Libya since she fled in 2011. "Although I do really want to go back," she said, "at the same time, my parents think we, especially my younger siblings, shouldn't because it may hurt the image we currently have of it. I have literally seen the rubble of the home I grew up in. But when I imagine home now, I do not think of that rubble. I just think of how it was before. I think of the serene nature and, as strange as it may sound, I really think of it as one of the most peaceful places I have ever been on Earth."

After all Maisara has gone through, she has resurfaced with a whole lot of grief but also a story—a story that has fueled her to desire to do what she can to advocate against the many injustices she sees in the world.

In the year after Maisara graduated from high school, she worked at Worldreader, the same organization I volunteered with the summer before.[74] "This experience exposed me to many areas, ranging from guidance on how to produce accounts for psychosocial predicaments and trauma all the way to market research and content translation into Arabic," she conveyed.

When Maisara attended university the following year, she decided to create the campus's first human rights club. Maisara formed this club to cultivate a "multidimensional approach toward understanding human rights–related predicaments through hosting frequent events spearheaded by guest speakers." Through these events, the members of this club created safe spaces for individuals who had been personally affected by blatant human rights abuses to feel comfortable sharing their truths.

In addition to her efforts on campus, Maisara now works with a grassroots nonprofit organization called Open Cultural Center in Barcelona. She helps lead a series of intercultural events put on by this nongovernmental organization to create spaces where migrant communities interact and share their stories with members of the community that hosts them. The main purpose of these events is to build awareness within the host communities of what migrants endure before and after they make it to a place of refuge. With this newfound understanding, Maisara and others hope that the host communities will do what they can to integrate displaced people into their societies.[75]

In addition to her school and other duties, Maisara is also a migration mentor for the BridgeBuilder Challenge 2019 for migration at OpenIDEO. According to OpenIDEO's website,

---

74   Worldreader. "Creating A World Where Everyone Can Be A Reader." [online] *Worldreader*. Available at: https://www.worldreader.org/ [Accessed 4 Dec. 2019].

75   Center, O. "Inclusion of Migrants and Refugees." [online] *Open Cultural Center*. Available at: https://openculturalcenter.org/ [Accessed 6 Dec. 2019].

the organization is "an open innovation platform that fosters worldwide collaboration to tackle emerging global issues through launching challenges, programs, and other tailored experiences."[76]

As a migration mentor, Maisara assists innovators in developing their proposals and projects by imparting validated, thoughtful opinions on how they may either serve or hurt the migrant community. Maisara reflected on what this position has done for her. "By working alongside a tremendously inspiring team of war survivors, refugees, and migrants to advance this challenge, not only did I find myself counting my blessings, but I also developed a greater sense of appreciation for the power I hold in impacting the lives of those who are going through what I went through."

Maisara reminds me of the strength I saw in Megan Ultimo, the dedication in Blythe Hill, and the advocate in George Freeman.

Maisara is them, and they are her.

Maisara endured the nefariousness of war and the fear of being displaced and seen as an outcast, but she has nevertheless persisted by dedicating herself to understanding "the ugliness of conflict in the hope of being a force in the journey of resolving it one day."

Megan, Blythe, George . . . Maisara. They are not just numbers. They are not just statistics thrown around to generalize the utterly non-generalizable. They are individuals who are tired of being hushed shadows in the stories that are so often discarded from being "too difficult to think about" or "too depressing to try to understand." No number involved in a human catastrophe is simply a number. It is a life.

---

76   Openideo.com. (2019). "BridgeBuilder™ 2019 Challenge: People on the Move." [online] Available at: https://www.openideo.com/challenge-briefs/2019-bridgebuilder-challenge [Accessed 6 Dec. 2019].

JUST BREATHE,
EVEN IF IT HURTS

———

Sometimes it's difficult to know exactly how to pinpoint the source of the angst and discomfort we experience. It can be unearthed from somewhere so far within you, exuding a certain unique quality in that it breeds uncertainty yet has undoubtedly been felt thousands of times before.

It's the tightness in your throat and the shortening of your breath. It's the sensation of repressed emotions crawling back up, latching on to every part of your body as they search for a place to surface.

You shift in your sleep, desperately trying to shake it loose, but its grasp is much too firm. So you give up. You give in to the moment and allow it to overcome you. You breathe and you feel. It feels so good to *feel*.

* * *

The first time I met Jeff Zlotnik, he told me and the others in the room that meditation is not an escape or a way to solve all of our problems. No, he told us. Instead, meditation will make us aware of the present moment and force us to confront our current emotions.

Jeff Zlotnik had been depressed since he was a teenager. He was miserable, as he puts it now, angry at the world for some ineffable reason. When he got to college at the age of twenty, one of Jeff's psychology professors saw how he carried himself and told him he ought to try meditation. Jeff commented, "Nothing else I was doing at that time was healthy or free. So I decided to try it out in my free time."

During his third year of college at the University of Arizona, Tucson, in 1995, Jeff began to volunteer at a group home for adolescents who had been physically and/or sexually abused. As meditation gave him some balance in his own life, he shared the practice with these individuals. "I would sit there with these kids for five minutes," he said, "and I would see these moments truly impact them . . . and knowing this, in turn, made a very long-lasting impact on me."

While Jeff was volunteering at this group home, he was taking a Chinese civilization class where he read a book that opened his eyes to a whole different realm of thinking called *An Introduction to Zen Buddhism* by D. T. Suzuki. This was Jeff's first introduction to the philosophy of Buddhism.

Jeff carried on meditating in a casual fashion for around eight years. Thinking about it now, he realizes he may have started to do it more because meditation and Buddhism was the hip, fun, trendy thing to talk about rather than for reasons of true personal resonance. In 2003, Jeff stumbled upon a local Taiwanese Buddhist temple in the San Diego neighborhood of University Heights. He went to a meditation practice there and left with an incredible feeling. He told them he would be back the next day—six months went by, and he never went back. Instead, he carried on with life as it had been since he graduated from college and got hooked up with a job where he was making more money than he knew what to do with.

One night, Jeff was in downtown San Diego with some of his buddies waiting in line to enter a club. "At this stage in my life, I had basically very little patience and a whole lot of money. When you live that lifestyle as a single twenty-four-year-old dude, living life downtown with a ton of money coming in, you tend to turn toward partying, or at least that is what I did. It is a pretty crazy environment," Jeff explained.

As Jeff and his friends waited, he lost his patience. He was about to pay the guard a whole bunch of money to let him and his friends through the VIP line when he had a disheartening realization. "I knew exactly how the night would end if I did this because it would be just like any other night: we would all get drunk, look for girls, and wake up the next day feeling like crap." Even after having this realization, Jeff proceeded to skip the line and entered the party, and his prediction happened. He woke up the next day and felt like crap. "My first thought when I woke up was, 'Shit, I got a headache.' And my second thought was, 'I need to go back to that temple,'" he commented.

For Jeff, that night was the turning point. Something inside him broke open, releasing the notion that he could not continue with this lifestyle if he ever wanted to be truly happy. "Yeah, I was having fun, but every morning I would wake up all alone and depressed. I started to wonder, 'Is this really what life is all about?' You know, the American dream—getting the money to get the stuff to fill the ego. And in the end, all it led me to was loneliness and sadness," Jeff expressed honestly.

Jeff had been doing the same type of consulting work from 1997 to 2003, about six or seven years of his life, and he absolutely hated it. "I don't necessarily regret or resent it," he stated, "but it was just . . . empty. There was nothing to it." Eventually, he began to spend a lot more time at the Taiwanese Buddhist temple in an attempt to center himself. For about two years, Jeff lived in a small place down the street from the temple where he would go to sit, meditate, listen, and learn.

One day, a Buddhist nun that was Jeff's direct teacher at the temple asked him if he wanted to move to their home monastery in the southern part of Taiwan called the Fo Guang Shan Monastery. Still trying to find a better balance and peace of mind, Jeff took them up on their offer and traveled to the small south Asian country in February 2005. He ended up staying at this monastery for nearly a year, until January 2006.

Jeff's experience in Taiwan was nothing short of mind-blowing. The very first day he showed up, one of the nuns showed him around. He was blown away when he realized that the monastery was huge. It could sleep around ten thousand people, so it wasn't a little temple in the hills. It was massive. It had very intimate, closed quarters where Jeff lived in the Buddhist college with the monks.

On the day Jeff arrived, it just so happened to be the Lunar New Year. There were thousands of people scattered around the space, seeming, somehow, to greet him in a joyous and glorified manner. The nun who showed him around told him something he will never forget. She said, "Jeff, when you get here, whatever you think you know, forget all of it and just be here."

Jeff took this little piece of advice and held it close, reminding himself of it throughout the years anytime his mind strayed elsewhere. He explained, "This allowed me to go there and not question or judge anything. I try to enter any unknown experience like this. And then later I can look back on it like, wow, what did that bring up in me? What was that like? What did I learn?"

For every day of the eleven months Jeff stayed in the monastery in Taiwan, he wore the same thing every day, ate whatever was in front of him, carried no wallet, no keys, no money, no phone, and just experienced life as it was. Not only were the simple daily practices he became accustomed to life changing, but the people he met also showed him an entirely different way of life.

When Jeff was in Taiwan, there were around twenty-five to thirty nuns who were studying in the English Buddhist college. These nuns were all being trained to go to the West to share Buddha's teachings in a way that would resonate with the life-style and general way of thinking of non-spiritually centered communities. The sweet nature of these nuns touched Jeff. "You know," he noted, "it's rare to be around a group of people who don't want anything *from* you. They are just living their lives with the purest intention possible. And that's rare. I would say that I learned more from the selfless way the monks and nuns lived than from the meditations or Buddhist teachings themselves."

Soon after his arrival, Jeff learned what it was like to wash his clothes in a bucket and a washboard by hand. He had two sets of identical clothing, one to wear while the other was drying from the wash. Every day, he would wake up at 4:30 a.m. and take fifteen minutes to put on his robe and brush his teeth. Afterward, he and the rest of the people living at the temple would walk in a line to the main shrine for morning meditation and chanting before breakfast.

One day while in the Taiwanese monastery, Jeff saw a man sitting and plucking his beard with a pair of tweezers.

Jeff, curious by this odd activity, politely asked the man what he was doing. The man replied simply that he was shaving. Through further conversation, Jeff learned that the man was from India. From the small village in India he was from, he never had a razor, and this is how everyone he knew shaved. So the next day, Jeff went into the stack of razors he had stocked up on from Costco before he left and gave one, along with some shaving cream, to the man with the tweezers.

The next day, the man walked around with a clean-shaven face and thanked Jeff. As he handed him back the unopened shaving cream, he said, "But what's this for?"

Jeff laughed. "It had never dawned on me that I hadn't explained to him what it was or how to use it." To this day, Jeff uses the cheap little blue razors that nobody ever wants to buy until they get rusty. And he thinks of that man every single day: how simple life was in his eyes, and how he never found something like plucking each strand of beard hair to be a hard or trying activity as most Westerners would. This man was one of the many individuals Jeff met in those months who never seemed to complain and instead found so much happiness and joy in the little things.

When Jeff returned to San Diego in 2006, his whole plan at that point was to spend the rest of his life building a bridge between Taiwan and the United States. He wanted to do this with the help of the Taiwanese temple in University Heights. However, he soon found out that this particular temple, like many, was very culturally oriented. Instead of trying to change the nature of this temple, Jeff shifted his goal to developing his own space to connect the West and the East. A few months after he returned, Jeff gathered a few of his like-minded friends. They were all sitting in a place downtown on a little red rug when the idea of the "Dharma

Bums" was first conceptualized. They adopted the name because of a few things they all enjoyed at the time: Bob Dylan, Jack Kerouac, and Buddhism.

From that one conversation on a little red rug, the Dharma Bum Temple was created and opened on December 31, 2006. For ten years, the Dharma Bum Temple was located where its idea was born: in a little eleven-hundred-square-foot loft in downtown San Diego. The Dharma Bums, as they called themselves, turned the downstairs into a social gathering area and a kitchen. The upstairs was eventually converted into a small place for meditation and dharma talks. And from there it flourished: a temple for the curious and the spiritually inclined.

In April 2017, the Dharma Bum Temple acquired a ninety-two-year-old church in University Heights and condensed both the Temple and a store called Buddha for You all under one roof. The Temple now welcomes five hundred to seven hundred people a week and all of their programs are free of charge.[77]

Jeff and his friend Maggie first took over the store Buddha for You in 2009. In 2010, they moved it next to the Vons near the campus of SDSU. Although it was not until 2017 that the store was donated officially to the Temple, Buddha for You's impact started as soon as Jeff and Maggie took over. They held small meditation and discussion classes in the back of the store for around four or five years. Gradually, more and more SDSU students showed up, mostly due to its proximity to campus.

Then in 2015, Jeff and a couple of SDSU students started to talk about creating a sustainable group centered around

---

77 Thedharmabums.org. "Dharma Bum Temple." [online] Available at: https://www.thedharmabums.org/ [Accessed 4 Dec. 2019].

meditation and Buddhist teachings on campus. Before they knew it, a few people who were passionate about the idea made it happen. Over the summer, this small group created a web page, logos, and other elements to form a real organization. They came up with the name that has stuck with the organization to this day: Delta Beta Tau (DBT—the same acronyms as its foundational temple, the Dharma Bum Temple).

One of the girls who was helping with this initiative wrote for *The Daily Aztec*, SDSU's school newspaper. During the summer of 2015, before the organization was even entirely in practice, she asked Jeff if she could write about the group, calling it a co-ed service fraternity based on Buddhist principles. Jeff agreed, honestly thinking nobody would read the article. About a week after the article was submitted, Jeff received a call from the *San Diego Union-Tribune* asking if they could interview him for a story on this new Buddhist fraternity. Jeff agreed, not knowing that soon after it would be picked up by Associated Press, spreading to national news.[78]

Soon he was contacted by KUSI, CW6, KPBS, and other networks.[79] "So I was getting all these calls and doing all these interviews in August 2015 when Delta Beta Tau hadn't

78   San Diego Union-Tribune. (2015). "SDSU could get first Buddhist frat, sorority." [online] Available at: https://www.sandiegouniontribune. com/news/education/sdut-sdsu-could-get-first-buddhist-frat-sorority-2015sep05-story.html [Accessed 4 Dec. 2019].; Leary, C. (2015). "Buddhist Greek life comes to campus." [online] *The Daily Aztec*. Available at: https://thedailyaztec.com/67846/news/buddhist-greek-life-comes-to-campus/ [Accessed 4 Dec. 2019].

79   Trageser, C. (2015). "San Diego State's Buddhist Fraternity, Sorority Aim To Bring Mindfulness To Mixers." [online] *KPBS Public Media*. Available at: https://www.kpbs.org/news/2015/sep/15/san-diego-states-buddhist-fraternity-sorority-aim-/ [Accessed 4 Dec. 2019].; KGTV. (2017). "Country's first Buddhist fraternity sits at SDSU." [online] Available at: https://www.10news.com/news/countrys-first-buddhist-fraternity-sits-at-sdsu [Accessed 4 Dec. 2019].

even fully launched yet. I realized I should probably talk to the school about it and let them know that this was even happening." Jeff laughed.

Therefore, Jeff scheduled a meeting with the dean of students. "And so I walk in and I'm all like, 'Hi. So I am Jeff. I'm the forty-year-old dude who's been sharing all this news about a fraternity that you know nothing about.'" He apologized, but ultimately the school was very supportive and encouraged the whole idea. That fall when school started up, Delta Beta Tau, the nation's first-ever Buddhist fraternity, was brought to life.[80]

* * *

I still remember what my first DBT meditation was like. I walked in with a friend of mine who was pledging that semester but didn't know anyone else. The joy and genuine love that took up every bit of space in that room was undeniable. I left that night in awe. I felt like I had just been hugged by a ton of different strangers, while in reality, I think I only spoke to one person other than my friend, and that was to ask if the seat beside them was taken.

I left that night overflowing with gratitude. I knew as I walked back to my freshman dorm that these meditations would be the calm I would need to stay centered amid the chaotic and ever-changing college environment.

I was introduced to DBT too late in the second semester of my freshman year at SDSU, so I was unable to pledge that year. However, I signed up to pledge in the fall semester of my sophomore year, 2018, without hesitation.

---

80 Deltabetatau.org. "Delta Beta Tau." [online] Available at: https://www.deltabetatau.org/ [Accessed 4 Dec. 2019].

DBT does not aim to convert college students to Buddhism. Although I am now highly active in this organization, I do not consider myself to be Buddhist. Instead, many other members and I are simply learning from Buddhist philosophies and indulging in a spiritual, not necessarily religious, path.

The DBT Pledge Program was founded on the six paramitas in Buddhism: generosity, morality, patience, diligence, meditation, and wisdom. The Pledge Program normally takes place over the course of ten weeks. Within these weeks, pledges participate in public Wednesday meditations and discussions, pledge meetings, retreats, socials, and community service opportunities. In the pledge meetings that are held every week, guest speakers come in to talk to the pledges about Buddhist teachings.

The four retreats were my favorite part of my Pledge Program. The first retreat is to the Dharma Bum Temple, bringing the pledges to the birthplace of the fraternity to experience a half day of silence. The second retreat, at the time that I pledged, was at a Zen Center in San Diego. However, due to the growing size of the pledge classes, this retreat location has since been moved to the Buddhist Temple of San Diego. The third takes the pledges about an hour north of SDSU to a beautiful monastery called Metta Forest. The fourth and final retreat is in Irvine at a Buddhist temple called Pao Fa.

Since DBT is still a relatively new organization, it continues to adjust to its growth every single semester. The primary community service activity that is offered is food distribution. We gather at one of the active members' houses on various Saturday mornings at 11:00 a.m. to make PB&J sandwiches. About an hour later, we carpool down to East Village to distribute the sandwiches and whatever else we choose to bring to the shelterless people. It is always a beautiful way to start off the weekend, to say the least.

Over the years, DBT has participated in many other community service opportunities, such as a program called Success Agents where some members go to a local elementary school to tutor at-risk students and forge meaningful relationships.[81] Every Sunday, DBT members lead small meditations and discussions with groups of high schoolers at the Dharma Bum Temple through a program called Dharma Bum Teens. In addition, DBT members have participated in animal outreach programs, cleaned up beaches and campuses, worked with the San Diego Food Bank, and most recently built homes for low-income families with Habitat for Humanity.[82] In 2019, executive member Jeanette Giovanniello created a show on SDSU's KCR Radio for members of DBT to get on the air to talk about how Buddhist teachings are applicable to their everyday life.

Another huge focus of DBT is on the biannual tradition of Mental Health Awareness Week. Although the tabling events have changed each year, the most recent string of events include Mindful Monday, where students learn about ways to ease stress; Take a Break Tuesday, where students paint with DBT and write down compliments on pieces of paper; Wind Down Wednesday, where DBT holds their weekly public meditation; Thankful Thursday, where written compliments

---

81 Justice.gov. (n.d.). "Success Agents." [online] Available at: https://www.justice.gov/usao-sdca/community-outreach-0/success-agents-2 [Accessed 4 Dec. 2019].

82 San Diego Habitat for Humanity. "New Volunteer? Start Here!" [online] Available at: https://www.sandiegohabitat.org/Volunteer/New-Volunteer-Start-Here?gclid=CjoKCQiAk7TuBRDQARIsAMRr fUat2HKGTHVJXqLWKwfG4T_c2obWxHdSxeqWbJjHzFkPBpzH_ kQUqtsaAnnPEALw_wcB [Accessed 4 Dec. 2019].

are handed out to people on the walkway; and Flexible Friday, where a yoga session takes place as a final act of relaxation.

Jeff often said that he created Delta Beta Tau because of how he struggled in his early twenties and wanted to form a place of refuge for people going through the twists and turns of college. DBT has become a place where individuals can ease their struggles, practice mindfulness, find refuge in a community, serve others, and better themselves as people. Although DBT is full of fun and exciting moments, it also can be for people suffering from grave or trying issues.

Mental health instability is one of the issues people face that is harder to identify than others such as homelessness or poverty. Every single person, whether they are extremely wealthy or can barely afford food, grapples with their mental health on a daily basis. We all have struggled to varying degrees with self-doubt, hatred, depression, anxiety, or whatever else it may be. Delta Beta Tau offers a place for people who struggle—which in my mind is every single person on this planet—to talk about what is hurting them and to come out of it feeling less alone and afraid.

By using Buddhist teachings as a way to guide conversation, we explore topics in depth such as patience, right-intention, impermanence, desire—scratching the surface of what we think we know and realizing how much we can discover. To me, the best part of these discussions and meditations and forged friendships has been the alleviation it has brought me. I realize I am not alone, others realize they are not alone, and together, we share joyous moments that relieve our suffering, even if temporary.

When people ask me about my experience joining DBT, I get a little taken aback as I recall how transformational it truly was for me. I found a home in DBT when I previously stumbled over my words whenever the question of "home" was raised. I felt comfortable, accepted, and loved in a very raw way. Finding DBT—this weird, interesting, cool group of people my age—was mind-blowing. Never had I imagined that on a college campus I would walk into a room full of students sitting in silence together . . . and actually learn to see so much beauty within it.

College, generally speaking, is made to be fun, new, and exciting. In a way, college offers escape: new things to try, new concepts to learn, and new people to meet. So many opportunities are provided to you in a confined space. However, when you leave college and enter your career field, escape can be more difficult to find. Jeff believes that what we are learning in DBT will help us so much in our lives here on out.

In Jeff's words, "When you're out of college, and if you find yourself in the mundane or routine life, what you learned in meditation and from Buddhist practices in DBT will become heavily applicable." I can only hope he is right, that we will be more mentally equipped to find peace wherever life takes us because we know that the cure to our negative emotions can be found within ourselves. It is and will always be accessible if we actively work on digging it back up.

Breathing meditation has become my way of dealing with life as it is, and, exactly as Jeff told me the first day I met him, it has been everything but an escape. In fact, I sometimes leave our active meetings or public Wednesday meditations feeling worse than when I first entered the space. The first couple of times this happened to me, I freaked out, blaming the practice for making me feel this way. But what I soon came to comprehend is that breathing in silence, the practice we do through DBT, is sometimes meant to be painful.

Our natural tendency as humans is to shut out our feelings. We push them far out of sight because we like to project to the world that we are strong and happy. Even if you do possess such attributes more often than not, no one person can ever be completely and utterly strong and happy in every moment. Silently breathing in a room full of other people who are doing the same leaves you no option but to think about all that is helping or hurting you. Sometimes the gravity of life is too strong and you simply cannot block out the thoughts and only focus on your in-breath and your out-breath.

This took me by surprise at first, but now I get it; feeling negative emotions *is* an extremely important part of the human experience. For without them, well, we simply wouldn't be human. I have learned that you cannot always push them away, because otherwise they will fester inside you, quietly awaiting their chance to flood your outer being. Instead, the practice of meditating in silence forces you to confront your emotions, feel them, and then, if you are lucky, release them.

When I asked Jeff what breathing meditation meant to him, he answered simply and without hesitation. "Well," he said, "What meditation does is it shows you that there is a point in time where you can just sit, breathe, and come to this present moment. Everything is beautiful just as it is, day in and day out."

There is a simplicity to it all, really. When you sit and breathe and focus on the present moment, you will realize that this moment too will pass, just like all the moments before it and all those after. And so will the emotions of grief, sadness, anger . . . despair. Just as negative emotions come and go, so will the positive. But by considering the magic of life and all the wonders it presents to every one of us, we can try to prevail with more love, kindness, and hope than their less delightful counterparts.

MAYBE

———

When I think about the feeling that activates my desire to work for the benefit of others, I like to picture a box.

I try to imagine my entire existence, everything that I am and that I am trying to be, fitting neatly inside this imagined cube. But the thing is, my mind simply won't let me. I see the unique parts of me ooze out of the sides of the box. I watch as my desired state of being creeps closer, following a thin line toward its epicenter.

As much as I try, the self-instilled rebel in me lashes out, displaying an array of arbitrary shapes and colors that represent my resistance to conformity. And then, shapes and colors that I cannot control jut outside the box and beg for the memory of the very things that broke me down and those that stitched me together.

Then I picture a box on the floor in front of my neighbor. I am surprised to see how easily my mind grabs each piece that surpasses the perimeter of their box and neatly folds it in. I crumble the shapes that do not matter to me and those that my mind has no capacity to see or to understand. As I look over my neighbor's box, I involuntarily compare it to my own. I only see the outreach of my own shapes and colors, not theirs. Upon comparison, I either become satisfied with the vibrancy of my own or saddened by its disarray.

It is in our inability to see the shapes of others, the elements that assemble who they are, that we fall into one of the three dangerous traps: egotism, pity, or jealousy. If we all taught ourselves to see through the thick, square lines of the boxes we have fabricated for others in our minds, our sympathy and aspiration to help others would surely elevate itself. When we stop thinking of those we aim to "help" as helpless on their own or simply confined to a number, our approach to aid can be positively altered. Then, with this changed mind-set, we can apply our desire to truly benefit others. Every single person we encounter has a totally new, intricate, and complex box, and recognizing that will allow us to see and understand the interconnectedness of the human race. Perhaps then we will be motivated to act upon our compassion to create elements of true change.

* * *

The individuals whose heartfelt stories are relayed through the pages of this book have pushed me down a path of surprising realizations. These individuals have taught me—both directly and indirectly through the way they speak about their journeys—that the process of *finding* meaning in our lives can be liberated with three simple efforts at the forefront of any of our endeavors: to show love to ourselves, transmit it to others, and take action when such love is not being generated so that our inner warmth can shine anew.

From this foundation, I reevaluated the meaning of both *success* and *happiness* in determining the quality of one's life. Before, I didn't realize the magnitude of the disillusion these words, particularly *success*, often create. *Success* is a shiny, deceitful word alluding to what we think we need to have or accomplish. It all too often succeeds in convincing us that it is an end line in which we will cross once we do it all "right." When maybe *success* is more like an oasis in the desert, consistently enticing us to chase after it, our lungs heavy as we struggle to breathe. The air thickens around us as all of the sand we've kicked up in our desperate chase clings to the humidity of the moment. We are all too often engulfed in this desert storm we create. We forget if we stop, if we sit down and give in to life as it is, ourselves as we are, we may begin to breathe again. And with our breath intact, we will begin to live again.

Like my previous illusory belief in the importance of determining my own story of success, I figured that happiness was the utmost goal of life, another finish line that I would cross once I had it all figured out. However, by interpreting the lessons outlined in the pages of this book, I began to view happiness differently. Maybe happiness is not a singular feeling to chase after but a glorified gateway to the process of becoming: a bending, twisting, conforming avenue that leads you closer to *you*, the person you are at your core.

And maybe shifting from the pursuit of success and happiness to the quest of simply living based on your present needs, desires, and the cries of those around you will truly lead you to a more fulfilling and meaningful life.

Maybe trusting the process, understanding your individual cause, and taking the actions necessary to follow through will make a difference in this dark, scary, and overwhelming world. Perhaps this altered mind-set will allow you to navigate the tangled paths that assemble your life, carrying with you the constant intent to see the good in all things.

Maybe, just maybe, this never-faltering ambition will allow you to find a way to let the glimmers of hope shine through the clouds of despair.

ACKNOWLEDGMENTS

___

I used to have a folder in Google Drive named "for the books I'll never write." To go from this mentality, this genuine belief that my dream of writing a book was nothing more than a fantasy, to actually publishing one, has been one of the most surreal processes of my entire life. Throughout this affair, I learned and expanded my views based on those I interviewed and extrapolated the falsehood of this mentality along with many others. I have condensed my interviewees' words, my interpretations of their lived experiences, into an inspired, raw look at what it means to live a life overflowing with meaning and how to find the hope in situations of despair.

Hopeful Despair would never have been written without an entire village of support. I am forever grateful and humbled by the love that has been shown to me by so many.

Thank you first and foremost to my family for supporting me every step of the way, always. Particularly during my preorder campaign, you all (especially you, Mom!) were the first to step up and help both emotionally and tactically.

Thank you to my marketing and developmental editors, Kristy Carter and Sherman Morrison, for your continuous ability to lift me up when I felt like giving up and for always prompting me with questions that permitted me to improve the quality and impact of my content. Thank you to my cover designer, Srdjan Filipovic, my co-cover design conceptualizer, Pola Mikulska, my copy editor, Christi Martin, my layout designer, Zoran Maksimovic, and everyone else who helped with the technical side of creating this book. And, of course, boundless gratitude for my publisher, Brian Bies, and the reason why I started this crazy journey in the first place, Eric Koester. You both are incredible forces of nature. I am truly blessed to know and to have worked with the two of you.

I would also like to extend a special thanks to the individuals who embody the purpose of *Hopeful Despair* and were courageous enough to retell their stories: Blythe Hill, Chris Temple, Marta Vernet, David Finklea, Michael Miner, Caroline Teti, Allie Knutson, Wendy Smith, Albert Manero, George Reginald Freeman, Seth Maxwell, Larsen Jay, Megan Ultimo, Steve Larson, Esra Ozturk, Aimee Halfpenny, Doniece Sandoval, Colin McElwee, *Layla and Hamid*, Jeff Zlotnik, and Maisara Sassi. You all inspire me in unique and monumental ways. I cannot wait until other people see you and your respective organizations in the way I do and always will.

Lastly, I would like to sincerely thank everyone (listed below) who gave valuable feedback, preordered the e-book and/or paperback, helped spread the word about *Hopeful Despair* to gather momentum, and ultimately helped me publish a book I am proud of. I am eternally grateful that you have given me a chance to share my thoughts with the world. Special human beings you are.

*Pam Skites

*Regina Sant'Anna

Jessica Nare

*Dan Skites

*Doug Skites

*Jeffrey Zlotnik

Emma Skites

Sofia Sant'Anna-Skites

Karli Reiter

Cooper Skites

Isabela Sant'Anna-Skites

Kyle Walsh

Sydney Wagner

Kylee Christiansen

Kajsa Wakamiya

Amanda Musolf

Shelby Betz

Will Robert

Witlie Leslie

Sarah Benchimol

Maria Marqués

Monica Alegre

Defne Sevil

Allison Lawrence

Madi Goodmiller

Hanna Griffiths

Jeanette Giovanniello

Alejandro Garcia

Maura Whiteley

Marta Marcos

Alexia Benchimol

Loryn Nieto

Pola Mikulska

Dillon Fuhrman

Spencer Garza

Leah Starr

Samantha Brown

Bailey Hahn

Diana Maria Crivtonencu

Cathy Cooper

Sherry Haque

Ahmed Naji

Emily Corson

Alex Donabedian

Molly Donaldson

Maya Parella

Gabby Thayer

Kika De Jong

*Kristin Brown

Nico Brennan

*Sherman Alexie

*Carrie Wirth

*Carolann Hochhalter

Carrie Whitacre

Marisa Schumacher

John Schultz

Karen Schultz

Lyla Omernik

Cathy Jo Prasnicki

Eric Koester

Kathy Jenkins

Kelly Schultz

Chad Reed

Ngaire Blankenberg

*Dorothy Balum

Lori Waldo

Laura McMillan

Brian VanDerBosch

Annie Volk

Michelle Faust

Marsha Hooley

Karen Wakamiya

Jose Juncosa

*Ron Mettler

Gerry Coleman

Denise Parks

Joe Schultz

Wendy Schultz

Mary Weller

*Lori Jurek

Kim Reiter

Linda Corral

Kathy Schulz

*Shelly Christiansen

Allison Davis

Lynn Nelson

Gwen Schewe and family

*Tiffany Penna O'Palick

Karyn Hahn

*Barbara Baines

Terri Hibbard

Erin Norrell

*Rachel Parsons

Mercedes Salvador

Maribel Domenech

Marilyn Bradley

*Marybeth Mataya

Lauren Schultz

Grant Schultz

Stacie Repsold

Daniel Repsold

Kolette M Brockhoff

*Marta Vernet

Mina and Arnold Mittelstaedt

*Valentina Pollini

*staff at the American School of Barcelona

Key
*multiple copies or campaign contributions

Made in the USA
San Bernardino, CA
24 February 2020

64891209R00122